# *Raising Happy, Healthy, and Holy Teenagers*

## A Primer for Parents

## Dr. Robert J. McCarty

Edited by Roxane Chlachula

National Federation for Catholic Youth Ministry
Washington, D.C.

**NFCYM**
NATIONAL FEDERATION FOR
CATHOLIC YOUTH MINISTRY

**www.NFCYM.org**

Robert J. McCarty, D.Min. is executive director of the National Federation for Catholic Youth Ministry. He has served in youth ministry since 1973.

NFCYM is grateful to The ACTA Foundation (Foundation for Adult Catechetical Teaching Aids) for its support of the printing of this book.

Publication Coordinator: Kathleen Carver
Text Layout/Design: Ruby Mikell
Cover Design: Ela Milewska

National Federation for Catholic Youth Ministry, Inc.
Washington, D.C. 20017

ISBN (paperback) 978-1-932619-03-4

First edition published 2001. Second edition 2009.

www.nfcym.org

# Table of Contents

## Raising Happy, Healthy and Holy Teenagers: A Primer for Parents

# Foreward

Teenagers! That word can strike fear in the hearts of many people. Bob's book *Raising Happy, Healthy, and Holy Teenagers* goes a long way towards eliminating that fear, and it actually gave us the realization that raising teenagers can be a rewarding experience. When we read Bob's primer, we constantly found ourselves thinking; "Why didn't we think of that?" and "That makes a lot of sense!" The book has straightforward examples of how to support and guide teens during an intimidating period of their lives (we especially liked Chapter 4). It definitely helped to ease our parental fear.

When our oldest son was in 9th grade, another parent volunteer in the high school youth group at our church told us she thought, "Matthew wanted to learn more and share more about his faith." Matt was in our opinion doing as much as we expected—attending school, a member of the school band and music ministry, attending church and religious education regularly. He was respectful, compassionate, drug free, and overall a very good kid. We learned Bob McCarty is so right. We can expect more from our teenagers. At first, we had no idea where to set the expectation; we had no idea Matthew was thirsting for more. He ended up getting involved in leadership team, going to summer work camp, service projects, and pilgrimages. He raised the bar for us and for the rest of the family.

This book is filled with so many truths that we wish we had known when our kids were young. You know the old adage—"I wish I had known then what I know now." We feel so lucky to have had someone literally tap us on the shoulder and point out that we can expect more.

Bob shares his years of experience and wisdom in dealing with teenagers in *Raising Happy, Healthy, and Holy Teenagers*. We have successfully used many of Bob's recommendations with our three teens—they actually look forward to attending church and religious education! As they get their driver's licenses and part-time jobs, we feel confident that we have prepared them to be responsible, well-rounded people. We wish we had first read the book when our kids were infants. We hope that you will let this book be your "tap on the shoulder" and that you will share it with your friends and relatives—especially ones with younger kids. It is a must-read for all parents!

*John and Debbie Mazzullo*
*St. Francis of Assisi Parish, Fulton, Maryland*

We got to know Bob McCarty well two years ago when he and his wife Maggie were our confirmation catechists. We were freshman in high school just learning how to deal with our new hectic life styles. Because of our constant involvement in activities outside of our home, we knew that we needed to give our parents constant assurance of our happy, healthy, and holy lifestyles.

When we began reading his book, we both knew it would be full of incredible advice that would create a better insight for both parent and teenager. Mr. McCarty did not disappoint us. The book clearly depicts the struggles teenagers go through in this day and age. We believe that if more parents got their hands on this book they would remember what it was like to be a growing teen and realize the differences we experience in our generation.

Throughout our time spent with Bob McCarty, we have realized just how much he understands the physical, emotional, psychological, and spiritual needs of teenagers. He is awesome when it comes to communicating with and relating to teenagers. As you can see, he has taken that talent and produced a wonderfully user-friendly guide to effective parenting. We truly hope that you will enjoy his wisdom as much as we have.

*Michael Mazzullo and Missy Mazzullo*
*St. Francis of Assisi Youth Ministry*
*Fulton, Maryland*

# Introduction

The following statement reflects the thoughts of many parents concerned about their teenagers.

> "If I can just get my kids through high school without their doing drugs, getting pregnant, getting hurt or getting into trouble . . . and if I could only get them to go to church . . . then I will be satisfied!"

With all the pressures and problems of our society today, many parents believe that these hopes are the most desirable and realistic goals for raising children. We all know enough young people who have been victims of any or all of the above situations to make these beliefs well founded. However, I am not ready to settle for just these goals for young people. I have worked too long with young people to believe that drug free, safe, chaste, and church going are all we can expect from them. These qualities are certainly important, but there is so much more in our teenagers. Teenagers bring an energy, an idealism, and a passion for living that is a gift to the adult world today. Young people have compassion and a hunger for justice that demands opportunity for expression. Lowering parental expectations of their children is not the solution. Having realistic expectations, while calling their children to something more in their lives, will ultimately better prepare their children for a healthy, happy, and mature adulthood.

Most of us who are parents do want something more for our children. The plethora of books and videos on raising children and the number of parents involved in their children's schools, community organizations, sports, dance, and music programs reflect the concern of so many parents. You are among those! Your willingness to simply pick up this book is a sign of your concern. You want to know more in order to be a better parent. However, your love and concern for your children is more important and will have more impact on how you parent than any book ever could.

The need for another book on parenting is arguable. However, my experience working with teenagers and their families over the past thirty five years has led me to believe that we could all benefit from a book on parenting teenagers that is simple, clear, and user friendly. As one who has parented for thirty-five years—my own daughter and various other young people who have come to live in my home—I know I have always looked for a new insight or another angle which would help me better understand my own daughter and all the other young people with whom I have been blessed to work.

Effective parenting is concerned with the whole young person: responding to their physical, emotional, psychological, and spiritual needs. An important focus of this book is assisting parents in meeting their teenagers' spiritual needs and fostering their growth in faith. Our children's faith development as adolescents is integral to the kind of adults they will become and the kind of life they will live. This dimension of parenting is very rewarding, even with the challenge of being a faith-filled person in a sometimes hostile secular world.

This book does not pretend to have all the answers. I write only from my perspective, heritage, background, and experience. There will always be a need for new insights on the parenting of teenagers as the situations confronting teens and families change. Our society is already witness to myriad configurations of family makeup. Families are two-parent, single-parent, step-parent, blended, interfaith, and multi-generational. Sometimes family membership differs from midweek to weekend. Families reflect their cultural heritage, customs, and traditions. The uniqueness of family situations makes parenting all the more challenging and highlights the need for approaches, techniques, and strategies which enhance the relationship between parents and their teenage children.

Not only can parents survive their children's adolescent years, but parents can enjoy, appreciate, and even cherish these years of intense growth, new insights, boundless energy, and excitement. This book, therefore, is written for the benefit of parents and children both, because children need their parents to be the best they can. Children need parental help, guidance, support, and nurturing as they move through their adolescent years, especially in a world where so many harmful and destructive experiences confront them.

The following chapters have been arranged in this manner:

- Chapter 1 addresses the situation of young people today;
- Chapter 2 describes the psychological and developmental tasks of young people;
- Chapter 3 offers some practical suggestions for improving parent-teen relationships;

- Chapter 4 discusses the concept of self-esteem and provides practical strategies for enhancing self-esteem in our teenagers;
- Chapter 5 examines the process of faith development in young people and provides suggestions for fostering the faith of our teenagers.
- The Appendix provides activities and sharing exercises which parents and teens can do together as a way of fostering understanding and communication.

Although the temptation is to skip right to the practical strategies in chapters 3, 4, and 5, a more worthwhile approach is reading the chapters sequentially. The strategies will make more sense if the reader first has an understanding of the context of young people: their situation today and their developmental tasks. So, on with the task and challenge of surviving and thriving with teenagers!

# Chapter 1

## *The Situation of Young People Today*

See if the following words describe any teenager you know:

> Our youth love luxury; they have bad manners; contempt for
> authority; they show disrespect for elders and love chatter in
> place of exercise. Children are now tyrants, not the servants
> of their households. They no longer rise when elders enter
> the room. They contradict their parents, chatter before
> company, gobble up their food and tyrannize their teachers.
>
> This quotation is ascribed to Socrates (469-399 B.C.E.).

Or consider this statement:

> I see no hope for the future of our people if they are
> dependent on the frivolous youth of today, for certainly
> all youth are reckless beyond words. When I was young,
> we were taught to be discreet and respectful of elders, but
> the present youth are exceedingly wise and impatient of
> restraint.
>
> Hesiod, 800 B.C.E.

And finally:

> The young people of today think of nothing but themselves.
> They have no reverence for parents or old age; they are
> impatient of all restraint; they talk as if they alone know
> everything and what passes for wisdom in us is foolishness
> in them. As for girls, they are foolish and immodest and
> unwomanly in speech, behavior and dress.
>
> Peter the Hermit, 1083 A.D.

Clearly, some characteristics of children and youth are timeless and universal. Certain aspects of the experience of living with children are shared by every culture and society throughout time. Even Scripture tells the story of Jesus wandering away from his parents while on a family trip and their not finding him for three days. And when they do find him in the temple, Jesus is nonplussed and seems unconcerned for his parents' anxiety. If this had happened today, Jesus' picture would have been on a milk carton! And we do not read anything else about Jesus until he begins his public ministry at thirty-years old. I suspect he was grounded by Mary and Joseph.

Parents do have to keep perspective about some of the behaviors of their children and avoid overreacting. However, the worlds of Socrates and of Joseph, Mary, and Jesus were very different than the world of young people today.

## Impact of Society

Children today are the product of a society and world experiencing rapid change. Advances in media, computers, and technology are coupled with sociological and political change. Children are becoming masters of the Internet and live in an age of instant experiences and virtual reality. Adults and children alike have front row seats as world events unfold on television, as evidenced by the millions who tuned into Pope John Paul II's last days and the election of Pope Benedict XVI. Families watched intently the coverage of September 11, 2001, the wars in Iraq and Afghanistan, terrorist attacks, civil wars in third world countries, and the horrors of ethnic cleansings. Families also witness the violence that seems to be escalating in cities, towns, and neighborhoods across the country every time they watch the television news broadcast. Global and local issues are brought into the family's living room every day and the bad news certainly seems to dominate any good news that might be happening. The concept of "the mean world syndrome" has been coined to denote the perspective of the world created especially through a media that concentrates on the bad news, coloring one's impression of current events and the world in which young people are growing up.

Our parenting styles are greatly influenced by our impression of the current climate in society. We seem to be raising our children to be more careful, even distrustful of the world around them.

We fear the possibility of our children being physically, sexually, or psychologically abused and so we teach our children to be untrusting of strangers, neighbors, political leaders, and even some religious leaders. We see the increase of drug and alcohol use, teen pregnancy, and the spread of AIDS and we try to be ever more vigilant and protective of our children. The world in which today's children are growing up is very different than the world in which we grew up. The adage "When I was their age" is itself outmoded. We were never "their age" in the sense of trying to come to maturity in a society that seems as threatening and unsupportive as the current situation.

Indeed, parents have every reason to be concerned about their children. We are so afraid that our children will be hurt physically, sexually, emotionally, or spiritually. Every time our children walk out the door, we ought to be saying a prayer for their safety. No longer are children's schools the safe havens we always assumed they would be. We do not send our children to their playgrounds without supervision. For some children, even their own neighborhood streets are not safe. We have become more careful about allowing our children to spend overnights at the homes of their friends, rightfully calling to check with the parents.

Children and teenagers have so many important decisions to make, so many factors weighing on them, so many opportunities for things to go wrong, it is a wonder that so many young people turn out okay. In fact, most young people do avoid the myriad pitfalls that seem to characterize adolescence. The volunteer rate among millennials—those young people born since 1982—continues to rise each year, now rivaling the volunteer rate of baby boomers according to www. VolunteeringInAmerica.gov (accessed 10/9/2009). They are going to college in increasing numbers, looking for work that will make a difference, and expecting to marry and have families of their own. Most become healthy and happy adults (just look

**They want to be happy, to get along with their parents, to have worthwhile occupations, and to be able to find meaning and make sense out of life.**

at us!) and young people overwhelmingly report loving their parents, valuing their families, and respecting their teachers. Clearly, many young people are surviving and even thriving. Why? Because they want to! Young people have a hunger to succeed in life. They want to be happy, to get along with their parents, to have worthwhile occupations, and to be able to find meaning and make sense out of life. And in order to support young people, we and the rest of society have to pay more attention to these hungers.

## Hungers of Young People

The following description of the hungers of young people comes from the experience of those involved in Catholic youth ministry. However, these hungers are generic to all young people, in all denominations and faiths. They may be expressed through a variety of behaviors, attitudes, and values, and in a language that is particular to a certain age group in a certain area of the country. But the experience of these hungers seems to be characteristic of young people growing up in our society today.

## The Hunger for Meaning and Purpose

Perhaps the great fear of young people today is that things do not matter, that there is no real meaning and purpose to their lives, their relationships, their future, their education or possible occupation. They look around society and see the quest for more possessions, wealth, and power and many young people wonder if that is all there is to life. Many youth are concerned about their future, wondering what kind of world will exist for them, what opportunities will be available, and whether they will be happy. Older teens ask questions about their place in this world and grow anxious about the type of occupation or vocation they will have.

Young people hunger for a sense of meaning and purpose. They do not want to just go through life, they want to have an impact, and they want to make a difference. In their youthful optimism, unscathed by the skepticism of many adults, teens are looking for something that provides meaning and value. Faith and a relationship with God should respond to this hunger by calling youth "to the fullness of their humanity, centered in God and expressed in the love of others." (*Catholic Youth Evangelization: Called to Be Witnesses and Storytellers* 5)

## The Hunger for Connection

Beginning with their experience of their family, young people express a need for belonging and connection on a variety of levels. Younger adolescents, generally those youth between 10 and 15 years old, are joiners, seeking out clubs, scouting, sports teams, and even gangs. The peer group and friends provide a sense of connection outside the home, even while, as older adolescents, they come to see themselves as connected to the larger communities of school, church, and society. Young people want a place where they fit in, where they are valued, where they are welcomed and accepted, and where "everyone knows their name."

### The Hunger for Recognition

Young people hunger for the affirmation that they are okay. Regardless of how secure they may seem outwardly, they want and need to feel worthwhile and important. They need to know that they have gifts and talents to share with others. Young people want to feel loved and appreciated, especially by their parents and other significant adults. Integral to this hunger for recognition is their need to be listened to, affirming that they have something valuable to say. Young people are crying out for genuine, positive attention.

### The Hunger for Justice

Teenagers have an innate sense of justice. Though the earliest expression of this might sound hollow to parents who remember "That's not fair!" the desire for justice, equality, and peace is very present in teenagers. Teens experience injustice, violence, hatred, prejudice, and even poverty—poverty of possessions and/or the spirit. They want to imagine a world where everyone has equal access to the goods and resources necessary to meet their basic needs. Many are quick to volunteer their time, energy, and talents on behalf of the less fortunate. They see the ills of society and they hunger to make things right.

## The Hunger for the Holy

Many young people today are searching for an authentic
experience of God. They see the gap between professed belief
and lived practice in their church communities, and they criticize
the apparent hypocrisy. "Young people continue to search for
a faith that makes sense, provides direction and meaning, and
that challenges." (*Catholic Youth Evangelization: Called to Be
Witnesses and Storytellers* 6) They want a religion that helps them
understand their experience of life with its joys and sufferings, as
well as enabling them to better articulate their experience of God.
And they want to be connected with others who are on this same
search.

We as parents and the rest of society have to address these
hungers in order to really foster the personal and spiritual growth
of teenagers and assist them in their journey towards healthy,
happy, and holy adulthood. The failure to do so will cause our
teens to go elsewhere in order to feed their hungers. Parents have
to honestly acknowledge the power of cults, gangs, and other
groupings to attract young people, in addition to the allure of
risky behaviors such as drinking, drug use, inappropriate sexual
relations, and crime.

Young people experience these hungers today as they
simultaneously grow to maturity in their families, in their
neighborhoods, and in the larger society. This growth to maturity
is an individual process that includes the successful resolution of
certain psychological tasks. The next chapter examines these tasks
more clearly.

# Chapter 2

## *Psychological and Developmental Tasks of Young People*

This chapter begins with identifying the internal, developmental tasks of adolescence, those tasks that are integral to this stage of psychological growth. The second part of the chapter describes the generation gap that is a natural outcome of the intersecting of adolescence and parents' middlescence, with some suggestions for bridging the gap that can develop between parents and teens.

The adolescence that is often romanticized in song, story, and proverb "These are the best days of your life" is a myth. Rare is the parent who would go back and do their teenage years all over again, unless of course, they could take the wisdom and learning of their adulthood with them. Perhaps the most accurate definition of this time of life is that adolescence begins around age 11 and goes until one recovers. The idea of recovering from our adolescence may be closer to the truth of what happens during this period of incredible physical and psychological growth. In a sense many parents may be "recovering adolescents" still coping with some of the turmoil and challenges of their teen years.

During this period of life, certain tasks must be accomplished or worked through. These tasks, often unknown to the teen actually experiencing their effect, can be painfully obvious to the observing parent. These internal tasks seem to combine during the teen years to create a time of explosions.

### Internal Tasks
Adolescence requires the handling of these five developmental tasks in order to foster healthy psychological development.

- Physical development
- Emotional development

- Developing a personal belief and value system
- Developing healthy relationships
- Developing a sense of individuality and personal identity

These tasks occur simultaneously, causing that much more confusion for the adolescent and challenging parents to greater sensitivity, understanding, and patience.

*Physical Development*
The first task during adolescence is to develop physically. During the years following the onset of puberty the teen's body literally explodes. Growth spurts are common and often painful. Many parents remember the experience during their own adolescent years of getting up one morning and looking in the mirror, either with hope or trepidation, to see what had happened to their bodies overnight. Teens can be so afraid of being physically too underdeveloped or over developed, too tall or too short, too heavy or too thin, too different or too much the same as their peers. Their concern is "Am I normal?" Their peers, who are grappling with the same concerns, are their points of comparison! They suffer from uncontrollable voice changes, hoping to sound more mature, but having to live with the sudden volume and tone changes. The onset of acne is probably the most painful sign of the physical changes occurring within their bodies. For many teenagers, acne is the most feared scourge, affecting one's self-image and one's ability to interact with peers. I can remember sitting in high school lamenting this adolescent leprosy and realizing that none of my teachers suffered from acne. That was the first time I allowed myself to believe that perhaps acne was an adolescent issue and that I might grow out of it, though this was little consolation in my immediate world. The problem is that there is no set schedule or pattern for physical development. For some, age twelve seems to kick off the growth spurt, while others are sixteen years old when their bodies change.

I can remember being 5'2" from eighth grade into my junior year of high school. Very little or no physical change at a time when my sister, who was two years younger, had already started looking sixteen years old while only thirteen. What an embarrassment to be mistaken for the younger sibling by strangers, teachers, and other teenagers. And at 5'2", with a body unsuited for most sports, I was a fast runner, which was essential for my survival, given my quick, verbal retorts used as a defense mechanism. In retrospect,

I know that I compensated for my size with a glib tongue and sarcastic wit that often put me in physical confrontation with my peers. Being able to run fast allowed me to live long enough to make it into my junior year of high school during which I grew seven inches in height. What an experience to have a body that was growing out of control. I went from being a fast runner to not being able to walk up stairs without tripping.

*Emotional Development*
Simultaneous with these physical explosions, the teen's emotions explode. They experience sudden highs and lows, intense moments of happiness and sadness, and wild mood swings. Learning how to name and express these emotions is the second task of adolescence.

In a parenting workshop a mother of three teenagers recalled her adolescence and described herself as a thirteen year old who had cried her way through the eighth grade. She remembered crying whenever someone spoke to her in the "wrong" tone of voice, and whenever no one spoke to her. And she did not know why. Parents are often surprised by the intensity of their children's emotional response to suggestions they make about their dress, requests for assistance around the house, or simple inquiries about school or friends. A youth's emotions are worn on their sleeve, ready to burst out with the smallest provocation. Knowing that their children's emotions are especially volatile during this period of development may help parents better understand many of the conflicts and arguments they might have with their children.

I remember having a conversation with my daughter, Shannon, when she was twelve years old. Actually, I thought it was a conversation, she thought it was a fight. I asked her why she was putting so much energy into this issue (long since forgotten), which I thought was fairly inconsequential (not a good attitude for me to have taken!), and she said, "Dad, I'm a pre-teen and I have to start getting ready." I could only surmise that she had either read the book or seen the movie on being a teenager and she was in training. Either way, this was an accurate foreshadowing of years to come.

Parents have to remember that no matter how illogical the strength of their children's emotions might seem (emotions are not logical anyway), these emotions are still very real for them. Anger, love, frustration, happiness, despair, joy, and loneliness are not right or wrong. Emotions are the signals that portray children's reaction to the surrounding environment of relationships, family, school, peers, and all the other dimensions of their life. A very important task for children, however, is to learn how to express their feelings in appropriate ways. Parents have to allow them to ventilate or share their feelings, and even more importantly, let them know that it is okay to feel whatever it is they are feeling. But be careful. Even though parents may understand how their children are feeling, we can hardly ever say, "I understand how you feel" or "I know just how you feel" or "I remember feeling that way too." Because for their children, the intensity of the emotions may be so new to them, that they honestly believe that no one could ever really understand how they are feeling, especially their parents. The best strategy for parents is to let their children have their emotions and assist them in naming how they are feeling. Often teens do not yet have the language to name the emotion they are experiencing. Teens and pre-teens will say, "I feel bad" or "I feel okay," not realizing that there are hundreds of descriptive words from which to choose. Naming the feeling is the first step in mastering its expression.

> **The best strategy for parents is to let their children have their emotions and assist them in naming how they are feeling.**

*Developing Personal Beliefs and Values*
A third task during adolescence is to develop a personal value
and belief system. Prior to adolescence the child relies on an
inherited value and belief system to provide a sense of meaning
and a standard for behavior. Parental values are their values.
But during adolescence or even earlier, they become aware that
not everyone thinks, acts, or believes the way their family does.
Teens are confronted by multiple belief and value systems in
school, on their playgrounds, on the sports fields, in the media
and through television. For example, issues like drinking and
drug use, cheating in school or in sports, peer relationships,
bullying, racism, and church involvement are handled differently
by different families and young people. It is important for parents
to clearly articulate their values with their children. It was not
unusual for me to say to my daughter, "We are McCartys and we
do/think/believe/act . . . this way." Parents should be explicit
about the values held by their family and expected of their
children.

However, teens do enter into an age of questioning and
challenging, trying to understand what they believe and why they
hold certain values. This is the awakening of their hunger for
meaning and purpose as described in chapter one. They may even
experiment with different beliefs and behaviors as they search
to find those values that help them make sense of their life and
future, and provide a sense of meaning.

This experience can be frightening for teens that have not had
an opportunity to discuss their beliefs, to put into words what
they believe, or who have never had to defend their beliefs to
a challenging peer. Chapter five will look specifically at how
faith develops during this time of challenging and questioning,
especially during adolescence, and the importance of parental and
adult modeling.

*Developing Relationships*
A fourth task for emerging adolescents is developing their
relationship skills. Younger adolescents often will claim to
have ten, twelve, or more "close" or "best" friends, while older
adolescents will identify only one, two or maybe three "close"
friends. Building upon the friendships of their childhood,
adolescents learn how to deepen relationships, experiencing new
levels of commitment outside their family, and expanding their

capacity for intimacy, resulting in fewer, but deeper friendships. This experience of intimacy, of interpersonal bonding first with peers of the same sex and then with those of the opposite gender, is a critical task since it foreshadows their later permanent, committed relationships like marriage. Within these relationships teens experience a sense of connectedness and belonging outside the family. These friendships are so very important to young people, often causing conflict when the teenager is asked to choose between family and friends. Parents sometimes have a difficult time understanding this bonding that occurs between adolescents, and sometimes parents just do not remember their own first "real" friends—those early "best friends" that marked their moving outside their family in order to meet their need for intimacy and belonging. This developmental task is enhanced or inaugurated by teen's exploding (are we getting the hint about adolescent development?) sexuality.

Sexuality is the impetus to intimacy and that gift from God that draws people into relationships with others. Most adults can remember how in elementary school the teacher could control behavior with threats of making misbehaving students sit next to the girls or boys—the opposite sex—which ever was the opposite! But somewhere in the later grades, around junior high age, this strategy no longer worked. In fact, sitting with the opposite sex became almost a reward. Suddenly students were forming relationships with peers of the opposite sex and were hanging around in mixed groups. Something had changed. Their sexuality had exploded. Junior high young people are likened to hormones on wheels with this new interest in dating, in one's physical appearance, and in the style of clothing one wears. All of this flows from this new impetus to relationships brought on by our developing sexuality.

When this task is considered along with the first task of physical development, the angst and anxiety that accompanies teen's physical development is very understandable. Suddenly during adolescence children's attention is focused outward towards the world of their peers rather than inward towards the family. This shift heralds the last internal task.

### Developing Personal Identity
Developing a sense of personal identity is a very important task and incorporates elements of the other tasks. Emotionally,

psychologically, and relationally adolescents begin to develop their own sense of individuality. For younger adolescents the great question is "Where do I belong?" or "Where do I fit in?" as they begin to distance themselves from their childhood influences of family and parents and begin to identify with their peers. Older adolescents begin grappling with the questions of "Who am I?" and "Who am I to become?" These are critical questions for developing adolescents and signal their move to a greater level of independence. How this move is handled by adolescents and by their parents has future implications for the relationship of parents and teens.

A helpful image for better understanding this process of individuation is to picture the family as a hand and each of the family members as fingers. Like the fingers on a hand, all family members are unique but connected to each other. During adolescence the teenager begins to pull away from the other family members in order to develop a clearer sense of who they are as an individual. Spreading the fingers apart enables each individual finger to be seen more clearly, even though they are still all connected. Sometimes this pulling away, this process of establishing one's independence, is slow and gradual and perhaps imperceptible to the parents. And sometimes this pulling away is loud and painful and looks more like rebellion than asserting one's independence. If we do not realize that this process is both normal and necessary, we might take it personally as a sign that our children do not appreciate our efforts, or do not love us anymore. We can feel frustrated and perhaps even doubt our parenting abilities. The signs of this stage of establishing one's individuality span the range from teen's selection of clothing, the new color of their hair, and wanting to spend more time with their friends to the risk behaviors of alcohol and drug use. Clearly, some expressions are more acceptable than others, but all flow from this need to set oneself apart from the very people who love them the most—parents.

Some perspective is provided by a popular saying often found on posters and cards that says: "There are only two things we can give our children that last: the first is roots and the second is wings." The roots are the experiences children have in their family and their relationship with their parents. The wings are these new expressions of individuality, of searching for one's own identity and one's place in this world. Sometimes parents miss the underlying psychological task that requires that all teens spread their wings at some point and parents might be tempted to cut off their children either figuratively or literally. Remembering the image of roots and wings and trusting the relationships that we have established with our children, we can trust that these roots will keep our children connected to our family, though in a new and more mature manner. Recalling honestly how this task of separating from our own parents was handled during our adolescence is a valuable insight. And though separating from one's own parents and developing one's individual identity is an adolescent issue, this task is often not accomplished during the teen years. Then the task of establishing one's own identity must be confronted later as young adults or adults . . . the "recovering adolescent" syndrome.

This process of separating can be a trying and difficult time for parents. But remembering that life is a series of separations is helpful. We need to remember back to when our child was an infant and we were holding their hands so they could walk. We knew that our child's first "official" step could only happen when the child walked without holding anyone's hand. We had to let go for our child to walk. And when we let go, our child would fall and have to get back up, and fall again and get back up again.

Then they go off to school and we remember the first time our children got on the bus by themselves, were dropped off at school, or were walked to their classroom and now other adults hold their hands through their times of learning. And as teens, they begin to challenge and even reject our parental guidance and values and we have to let go even as our children pull away and emerge into semi-adults with their own views, friends, and values.

Throughout the lives of their children parents offer both their love and their control, but, beginning with adolescence, parents should gradually loosen their control, and that's very difficult. We need to remember that love and control have to be different with teens than it is with children and that though teens outgrow their need for control; they never outgrow their need for our love.

Adolescence is a period of testing—of testing parents, school authorities, and church. Adolescence is a time of establishing one's independence. Sometimes, though, youth proclaim disbelief in old teachings—those of parents, school, and church—and profess unconventional or counter-cultural opinions (anything different from what their parents hold) as a hasty declaration of freedom. Sometimes it is more for shock value than out of genuine conviction. Often, they are just looking for our reaction. The wise course is to take most of what teens say and do with a grain of salt, knowing that they are searching and experimenting. Unless of course their experimenting has harmful consequences, as in the case of drinking, sexual activity, and risk behaviors, when a more direct and immediate response by parents is required. This situation will be further addressed in the next chapter.

We must remember that however much our teenager comes across as self-assured; the fact is that these multiple physical and psychic explosions undermine self-confidence. The adolescent feels considerable anxiety and insecurity. This is expressed in some teens by a withdrawn shyness, while others disguise this nervousness with false bravado. At age eleven children can seem so confident and secure, and by age fifteen or sixteen they can be so confused and anxious.

## The Generation Gap: Whose Creation?

Parenting teenagers would not be nearly so difficult if we, the adults in the family, were not also going through our own developmental changes. We do not always like to consider the fact that we never stop growing. Most theorists dealing with human behavior postulate a series of stages that people progress through in some sequence, whether it is in the moral, cognitive, faith, or psychological realm. Even popular conversation has become more comfortable talking about life's passages or stages. Often though, beliefs about life's developmental stages are couched in humorous warnings about "turning thirty, forty, fifty" or "retiring at sixty-five." At whatever age, even "over the hill" minimally implies two stages of life; climbing up the hill and coasting down the other side. Adults intuitively know that they continually develop, confronting new life tasks as they do so. So, what happens when the developmental growth of adult parents coincides with their teens' adolescent explosions? A generation gap is created.

> At whatever age, even "over the hill" minimally implies two stages of life; climbing up the hill and coasting down the other side.

Simultaneous with children entering adolescence, many parents enter middlescence, that life stage that occurs somewhere between thirty-five and forty-five years old. The developmental tasks of each stage often conflict in four areas: identity, physical development, independence, and intimacy and family.

### The Great Identity Question

For adolescents, the question is "Who am I?" as they begin their search for their individuality. Simultaneous for many parents of teenagers, the question is "Who am I now?" Now that the children are becoming more independent, getting themselves to school, dressing themselves, and choosing their own friends, the parents' role must change. Even more drastic, as the last of the children graduate from high school and move out of their house, how will parents handle the "empty nest syndrome"? Or "who am I now that I am a grandparent?" The more the parents' self-definition and identity is determined solely by their relationship with their children, the more difficult this new question: "who am I now?" If we only know ourselves, or if our spouse and children only know us as mother or father, when that role diminishes (though it never entirely disappears), then the question "Who am I now?" requires a new answer.

This great question is the impetus to the further development of identity. For adolescents, this is a time of an ever expanding self, trying out new values and beliefs, determining goals, expanding one's circle of friends. For us, middlescence is often a time of consolidation in terms of career, goals, and our definition of success. For the teenager the future seems boundless and open, everything seems possible, while we become painfully aware of this age of limits. We realize that we are not going to achieve everything we thought we would (back when we were teenagers). Often a move towards a more conservative lifestyle occurs. We become more conscious of retirement accounts just when our teens are so thoughtlessly spending all their own money (or our money!) on their next whim. Parents and their teenagers seem to be heading in different directions.

### Physical Development

One of the built in traps of adolescence is teens' false sense of immortality. They feel young, healthy, and strong and that they can do it all. They feel they have so much life to lead. After all, their future is far longer than their past. Many feel that nothing can hurt them. This reasoning becomes very dangerous when it serves as the basis for teens' decisions about experimenting with drugs and alcohol and sexual relationships. Some young people feel that their bodies can heal themselves, that they are strong enough or healthy enough to withstand the physical costs of using alcohol and drugs or engaging in inappropriate sexual relationships.

Experiencing the death of one of their peers is a powerful shock, whether through an accident, an illness, or as the result of suicide, because of the myth that "teenagers are not supposed to die." Teens experience themselves physically as getting stronger and taller, and often there is little concern about caring for their physical selves. With the possible exception of young people who are involved in athletics, adolescents are the group with the least commitment to regular exercise, because their bodies do not require the same level of maintenance.

We experience something different. During middlescence we begin to confront our physical limits and perhaps for the first time, experience a fear of aging. On turning forty years old, my daughter reminded me that I was entering the "age of Bermuda shorts and black socks" and that she had noticed that I was "packing on some pounds." As a fairly dedicated runner and basketball player, this was not easy to hear from this teenager who would not know regular exercise if it bit her on her couch potato. But the words ring true, even more so now that my doctor has forbidden any running because of a damaged knee. If we are finding ourselves in one-on-one competitions with our teenagers and we are not quite ready to lose gracefully, then this is a familiar reality. Physically, parents and their teenagers are heading in different directions.

And without going into too much detail, physical development is related to the physical expression of one's sexuality. At a time when a teen's sexuality is bursting, we often find the individual rethinking his/her sexuality—or at least thinking more about sex. As a male I cannot fully appreciate this statement by a woman friend who described menopause as "standing in the supermarket and crying over the broccoli." I suspect, though, that sex and sexuality is an issue that needs addressing in this time of middlescence for both men and women.

## Independence

As previously described, the teenage years are characterized by a growing sense of independence. As teens struggle to appreciate and establish their own uniqueness, they pull away from the family and, therefore, from their parents. This movement often parallels the parents' growing need to be needed. Somehow, when children are very young, their need for parents is so clear that it is not even an issue or concern. But suddenly, when we are not needed in the same way, we want some reassurance of our importance to our teenage children. We may want what our teens are unable to give—or at least unable to admit—that they need us. Certainly, this issue is more or less obvious to us, depending on our family and our previous relationship with our children. But acknowledging this need is a further example of how parents and their teenagers are moving in different directions.

## Intimacy and Family

Perhaps the most common cause of tension between parents and teenagers revolves around family and family time. Just when our teenagers are moving outside their family in order to develop deeper relationships with their peers and to begin experiencing intimacy, we are often trying to recapture or reinforce a strong sense of family. When I was in elementary school, my father worked several jobs, often preventing him from being home at dinner time. When I reached high school, my father changed jobs and was now home at a regular time. This occurred as I jumped into a pattern of playing sports with my neighborhood friends every day after school and into the evening hours. There was no place else I wanted to be but with the guys playing ball. My father's announcement that each dinner was to be a family meal requiring my attendance became a source of major conflicts between us.

Families will experience this tension in different ways. Our teenagers ask to vacation with their friend's family instead of going on the annual family trip. They have something else to do whenever a visit to a relative is planned. They want to have dinner with their friends. And this situation worsens when they start dating. Now they want to spend all their time with their girl or boy friend. Christmas traditions and birthday celebrations are challenged. The quickest way to start an argument is to say,

"But we've always done it this way." If family celebrations and gatherings have not been the norm, trying to newly create this sense of family as our children move into adolescence will be a struggle.

For teenagers, this impetus to peer relationships is very exciting. They are experiencing intimacy outside the family, perhaps for the first time, and they feel very adult-like because they are doing the choosing in terms of friends. This newfound intimacy points to another source of conflict which will be addressed later—our teens' friends.

These issues lead to a natural generation gap. The simultaneous emergence of adolescence and middlescence, in both their differences and similarities, creates a tension that is normal and survivable. Recalling the previous chapter, young people need to put distance, a gap, between themselves and their parents. They have to learn how to function independently and develop their personal self-identity. Teens must forego total and comfortable dependence on their parents in order to become responsible adults. But this standing on one's own causes anxiety and fear, even as it feels exciting. We, then, have to suffer the pangs of separation and the anxiety of our children making this transition without getting hurt. We live with our doubts, "Did I do a good job of raising my kid?"

In the midst of this gap, teens are getting signals from a new and powerful source: their peer group. Because of this movement outside the family for significant relationships, the peer group challenges parents (and teachers) for the allegiance of the young. However, in this move outside the family for acceptance and affirmation, young people also feel the loss of closeness with parents and other adults who are special to them. They are pulled in two directions: the unchartered waters of independence and the safeness and security of old ties. Often, their rude, sullen, and argumentative behavior is a desperate denial of their wish to remain close.

A delicate balancing act exists for parents who support and allow the pulling away by their teens when it is safe and appropriate, while holding their arms wide open for when their children want to return to the comfort of home. If we do not understand the psychological task that underlies our children's behavior, their pulling away and wanting to be close, then we may take their pulling away as rejection and not allow for their wanting to be close. "You made your bed, now you have to lie in it" is a phrase that captures a faulty understanding of what is going on. Like the father in the parable of the prodigal son, parents must wait and watch for the "lost son" to return home. And this may be a daily routine.

Having explored these areas of concern, the issue of teens' pulling away and risk behaviors needs closer examination. We need to distinguish between symbolic rejection and real rejection. The need for teens to push against parental beliefs, values, and even rules in order to establish their own sense of individuality and independence is developmentally normal. This period of testing is more symbolic rejection when the means of testing and rejecting include clothes styles, haircuts, music, or other fads.

This testing becomes far more serious and even dangerous when the means include drinking, drug use, sexual experimentation, running away, threatening suicide, and delinquent activities. These activities are far more real rejection and are problem behaviors. Parents have to be able to distinguish between disturbing behaviors and disturbed behaviors. The latter activities are disturbed behaviors and require professional intervention. And just a note of caution. Since families are like a hand (to bring back a previous image), what affects one finger, affects the entire hand. So one child exhibiting disturbed behaviors affects everyone and should be treated as a family issue, not just the individual child's problem. Not only will the acting-out child benefit from our support and concern, but perhaps we will uncover some unconscious ways we are contributing to the problem situation. If we truly love our children, then we have to risk our culpability and become vulnerable and open to change.

Choosing to enter family counseling is a sign that the entire family, parents included, is both concerned about the situation and committed to seeking shared solutions, rather than passing blame on one person. We can contact school counselors, parish ministers, or local community social services for referrals, if counseling seems appropriate and necessary. We should contact the referred agency or counselor and ask them questions about their approach, experience with adolescents, fee structure, and availability. Counseling creates an opportunity for the family to address the issues causing disruption and concern, and also provides support for both the parents and their children as they struggle with new ways of behaving and relating with each other. The willingness to honestly deal with family issues through counseling really is an investment in the future of the family and a commitment to developing healthy family relationships.

## Bridging the Gap

Even though this generation gap is normal and even developmentally appropriate, effective communication and good relationships with our children are still possible. In order to bridge this gap, however, both we and our teenagers must be willing to let go of some things, and also willing to build something.

The letting go is a shared task. We and our adolescents must let go of some assumptions, if a good relationship is to be developed. These assumptions will be examined as they exist in both the adult and teen sphere.

| Parents | Teenagers |
|---|---|
| "We have all the answers" | "My parents are experts" |
| "We have all control" | "Convenient dependence is okay" |
| "We are still their hero" | "False innocence and ignorance is an excuse" |

### We Have All the Answers . . . My Parents Are Experts

First, we have to let go of "having all the answers." Wanting to be the supreme source of knowledge in every area of our teen's life is a natural parental temptation. When children are younger, appearing "all knowing" is easier for parents because children's questions and concerns are more basic. And because we start out by appearing to have all the answers, we sometimes assume that's how it will always be, or that is how it is supposed to be. This is a myth. As children move into adolescence and more into the realm of school and peers, their questions become more complex. Not only were parents "never their age" because of the changing societal context in which teens now grow up and, consequently, we do not necessarily have the answers, but teens also need to struggle with finding their own answers. Even when we do know the answer, the better course might be for our teens to search out their solutions. We can offer guidance, different perspectives or points of view, and even possible options for their dilemmas, but only when asked, and even then, with a degree of humility, for we have now become advisors. Whether the issues concern dating, peer relationships, school concerns, employment, faith, or religious questions, we have to let go of having all the answers. And more importantly, we need to cultivate the skill of asking the right questions. For then, we can guide our teens' thinking processes, raise issues our teens may not have considered, and express our own concerns, without becoming judgmental, overbearing, or intrusive.

The following questions are appropriate for a variety of situations and are designed to enable the parent to guide their teen's decision making process. There is a decision making model provided in the appendix of this book.

- What do you want for you? (In this situation)
- How are you feeling about this situation?
- What options or alternatives do you have?
- What are the possible consequences of these options?
- Which option seems the best to you, given what you want for you? How would it feel to choose that option?
- What do you need to do? (To get what you want for you)
- Will you do it?
- When and how will you do it?
- Will you let me know how it goes?

With practice we can learn to add other questions, depending on the situation or issue being discussed. The underlying key is to enable our teen to identify the issue, options, and solution, and thereby create ownership for the solution and outcome.

If we have to let go of having all the answers, teens have to let

> **The underlying key is to enable our teen to identify the issue, options, and solution, and thereby create ownership for the solution and outcome.**

go of thinking "parents are experts." Of course by the time our children enter into adolescence, many of us have already received the message from our children that we are no longer the experts. In fact, children often roll their eyes in disbelief of how little parents seem to know. Mark Twain once commented that when he was sixteen years old he could not believe how stupid his father was, but by the time he was twenty one, he could not believe how much his old man had learned in five years. So, thinking that we are experts may be an easy myth for teens to let go.

However, teens have to realize, especially when they are most frustrated with us, that we have received minimal training for this role of parenting. We may be educationally degreed, occupationally professional, and mature adult people, but where did we learn how to be parents? We do not take courses and receive certificates of competency. What is the primary source of most parenting knowledge? Our parents. Very often we find ourselves imitating our parents, using their techniques and even repeating some of their parent-like statements, despite all oaths to the contrary. But what happens if our parents were lousy parents? Many adults who are now parents themselves grew up with parents who were not always present to them, or loved them the way they needed to be loved, or related to them in supportive ways. Perhaps our parents could not be effective parents because they never learned how, or because their lives were too chaotic.

Or what happens when the current generation of children has needs and issues different from those of their parents and, therefore, they require different parenting skills or approaches? How are these new skills and techniques developed? Usually, we practice on the first born child! The first born is often referred to as the experimental child because parents are trying out their parenting techniques. Adults who are the oldest child in their families all have stories of how differently they were treated than were their siblings. Another technique for learning parenting skills is to read books like this one and watch our peers parent their children. Children have to accept that we are struggling to be the best possible parents, which means that mistakes will be made. And children must realize that our mistakes are born out of our love and concern for them. We will never be perfect, but we can be the best possible parents with practice and our children's patience.

*We Have All Control . . . Convenient Dependence Is Okay*
Second, in order to bridge the gap, parents have to "let go of their kids by lessening their control." We cannot expect to have the same control over our teenagers that we did when they were younger children. In fact, it is not healthy for teens to be treated like children because they never have the opportunity to develop their own life skills. Just as too little control leads to no sense of self-discipline and structure, too much control will suffocate teens. Simultaneous with our lessening control, teens have to "let go of dependence." It is very reasonable to assume that teenagers will begin to take care of themselves, making personal decisions, and

handling their personal tasks and responsibilities. Basic matters of getting themselves up for school, completing their homework, making sure they have clean clothes, and being responsible for their schedule are all examples of moving from dependency towards independence. Obviously, this move does not happen magically upon one's thirteenth or sixteenth birthdays. Rather, personal responsibility is increased gradually throughout their grade school years, so they can develop the necessary skills for adolescence. Teens become less dependent as they learn and utilize their skills for decision making, problem solving, time and stress management, conflict management, developing friendships, and maintaining healthy relationships. The following are areas where parental control can be lessened as teen's responsibility increases.

- When to do homework
- When to do household chores
- Responsibility for specific household chores
- Getting oneself up for school
- How to keep one's room
- Buying one's own clothes
- Applying for a job
- Choosing a college and a major
- Choosing participation in extra-curricular activities
- Having a car, or use of the family car
- Involvement in church youth programs
- When to begin dating
- Curfews
- Determining bedtime

Using the sample questions previously provided, we can assist our children in making good decisions about these basic areas of their lives. This also teaches the skill of effective decision making which will be very important for children and teens as their decisions become more serious. When my daughter was in first and second grade, I would ask her when she came home from school whether she wanted to do her homework before dinner, which allowed TV time afterwards, or after dinner, allowing for playing outside prior to dinner. The question was never, "Do you want to do your homework?" It was "when." I controlled that she would do her homework. She controlled when she would do her homework, learning decision making skills by choosing among options after considering the consequences. In high school, she had much more control over if and when she did homework, and when she was in college, I did not have any idea how, if, or when she did homework, and I am not sure I wanted to.

The previous examples describe areas where our children can begin learning basic skills, while we lessen our control and they lessen their dependence on us to solve all their problems and handle all their needs. The following graph illustrates the relationship between parental control and children's age—or the movement from children being dependent to independent and finally interdependent.

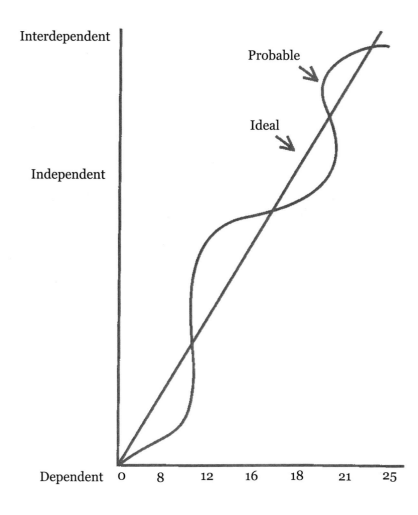

We should discuss together with our children where on this graph we handled the responsibility for choosing music, buying clothes, choosing their school, keeping a budget, interviewing for a job, choosing an occupation or college major, and making decisions about sexual involvements. And at what age would we see our young person making these decisions?

If we foster our child's dependency too long, becoming overprotective, we run the danger of creating the eternal child. The young person who has never had the opportunity to make any decisions that affect him or her, the one who has all their needs met by their parents, and the one who has never had to become responsible, only learns dependency. They, figuratively, are not allowed to grow up, because they are kept as a child by their parents. The eternal child develops into a very immature adult and has difficulty achieving any kind of healthy independence.

The opposite, however, is also a danger. Children who are forced by their circumstances or their parents' choice to grow up too quickly are often referred to as hurried children. These children take on adult responsibilities early in life, such as managing the household or being the primary caretakers for their siblings. Often, because they have become accustomed to adult roles, hurried children begin experimenting with other adult behaviors, such as drinking, smoking, and sexual relationships. They become independent before they have had the opportunity to develop some of the life skills necessary for adulthood, such as responsible decision making, identifying the possible consequences of one's actions, ability to fulfill commitments, and the ability to develop healthy relationships. Sometimes, the hurried child has "done it all" by mid-adolescence, and they are left with little to look forward to in adulthood.

Letting go of control is a gradual process that respects our teens' growing responsibility for themselves, their personal maturity, and their self-reliance. Holding control too long can suffocate children, while letting go too soon can cause children to drown.

---

**P**eople are born talkers, but genuine communication is a learned skill.

The parental decision to loosen control must be related to their children's ability and willingness to assume personal responsibility and requires that we have the ability and an openness to negotiate with our children.

*We Are Their Heroes . . . Innocence and Ignorance Is an Excuse*
The third myth that is best let go in order to bridge the gap is the desire of "wanting to be their hero." This myth is related to the first myth of having all the answers. We just love that time of childhood when our children are younger and they think we are wonderful and perfect. We are the smartest, most talented, and all around best people our children know. We are the protector, the wise sage, and the provider for the family. And being up on that pedestal does feel good, however brief the stay there. We soon go from being the most admired person in our children's life to being outdated. Our children's allegiance is transferred to the current rock star, athlete, or movie star. The picture of us hanging in their bedroom is replaced by someone else. We have only to look at our children's bedroom walls in order to know their new heroes.

And while we let go of being the hero, our children must let go of their false innocence and ignorance. Though we are no longer the great protector and sage, our teens make a mistake if they now look towards those other new heroes as their role models, after whom to pattern their lives. Teens have to let go of their ignorance around issues of drug and alcohol use, inappropriate sexual activity, and irresponsible driving. The "it cannot happen to me" syndrome is a myth, a false assumption. Drug addiction, alcoholism, pregnancy, sexually transmitted diseases, and accidents do happen to teenagers. They certainly have the right to good, accurate information about these risk issues, but they also have the responsibility to consider these issues carefully. "I did not know this could happen" reflects false innocence and ignorance.

*Communication Skills*
So, bridging the generation gap requires that both parents and teenagers let go of their false myths. But just letting go of false myths is not enough in order to develop a better relationship. There has to be something put in its place. We and our teens are challenged to build a new relationship, based on effective communication, mutual respect, and trust. Communication is a common issue for all families, as evidenced by the number

of books written on the subject. People are born talkers, but
genuine communication is a learned skill. Here are five practical
communication skills that will enhance our relationship with our
teens.

- Listen, listen, and listen
- Paraphrasing
- Avoid "either/or" statements
- Use effective body language
- Use appropriate tone of voice

The time that we spend in practicing these skills will be invaluable
in fostering an open relationship with our teenagers. In the
appendix of this book, Exercise #5, "Do Not Say . . . Do Say!" is a
good activity to use with our teens for identifying sentences that
either help or hinder communication.

### Listen, Listen, and Listen
And listen some more. God gave people two ears and one mouth
so that we would listen twice as much as we talk. We need to listen
to our children, and it is probably the most difficult when they are
teenagers and we disagree with what they are saying. We often
fall into the trap of planning what we want to say while our teen
is still speaking. This means we do not really hear all of what our
teen is saying. Listening takes energy. We have to really focus on
what our child is saying. Understanding what our child is saying
is the goal of effective listening. Understanding is not the same as
agreement. We may not agree with what our children are saying,
but we should work for understanding.

### Paraphrasing
The sign of genuine listening is the ability to repeat back not only
what the child says, but also how they seem to feel and why. A
sample formula is "You seem to feel . . . when you . . . because . . . ."
For example, "You seem a bit overwhelmed when you talk about
your school work because there is so much to do." Or "You seem
pretty angry when I ask you to do your chores because you do
not think I am being fair." The formula is not as important as the
pieces: feeling, content, and reason. When all three pieces can be
identified, genuine listening and understanding is taking place.

### Avoid "Either/Or" Statements

A common parental approach to an argument may sound something like "Either you do what I say, or you are grounded forever." And the natural inclination is for teenagers to see how long we can stand them around the house. We should never say "either you . . . or . . ." unless we are ready and able to carry out the "or." These statements really box us into a corner, giving us only the option of carrying through on the consequence or losing respect. A more effective approach is to give our children options and thereby enable them to develop their decision making skills. So, instead of "Either you cut the grass today or you are in for the weekend," a better question might be "On which day would you rather cut the grass?"—which is not to say "Do you want to cut the grass?" Giving teens options and choices within some parameters, gives them control over the use of their time, and teaches them about decisions and consequences.

### Use Effective Body Language

When talking with teens, do not do something else that is distracting, like reading the paper. We demonstrate that we are giving full attention to our teenager by maintaining good eye contact, facing our teen, and leaning forward if either is sitting down. Nonverbal support and encouragement by giving a smile, a hug, a wink, a pat on the shoulder, nodding the head, or reaching for the child's hand is very important. Body language is even more effective than the words used when communicating, so we should pay attention to what our body language—and conversely, what their body language, is communicating.

### Appropriate Tone of Voice

The tone of voice is very important in effective communication. Our tone should not come across to our children as sarcastic, all knowing, or even disinterested when responding to our children or when our children are sharing something with us. Our use of encouraging phrases with a genuine tone of voice demonstrates our interest and keeps the conversation going. Phrases that are helpful include "And then what happened? What did you do next? How did that feel? Tell me more about that."

This chapter has described the internal developmental tasks of young people, the natural generation gap between parents and teens that is created, and ways of bridging this gap in parent-teen relationships. Additional strategies will be described in the following chapters and various exercises and activities are provided in the appendix.

# Chapter 3

## *Practical Parenting: Giving Youth Roots and Wings*

The following tips have been developed through conversations with parents and with teenagers and provides some guidelines for setting family rules, handling consequences, and developing relationships.

### Strategies and Guidelines

*Recognize Teens' Need for Stable Rules*
Everyone needs to know the rules, whether it be in the home, at work, in school, or in society. Teens benefit from stable rules. During adolescence when they begin to experiment with their own individuality, they need something to rebel against. Pushing against parental rules is natural. In the approach to exercise called isometrics, a person pushes various muscles against an immovable object in order to develop that muscle group. Family rules provide the object against which adolescents push, in order to develop their inner emotional, psychological, and personal muscles: their sense of right and wrong, appropriate and inappropriate behavior, following directions and learning obedience. But if every time they push, the rules collapse, then they do not learn anything. They do not develop any inner strength.

So the rules must be stable, but that does not mean they have to be rigid and unchangeable. For example, even though a teen's curfew is usually 10:00 PM, on the night of a special school dance the rule might be changed to a later time. Now, that does not mean that the rule has to be changed for any or every reason—every request is not a "special" event. However, rules should be flexible depending on circumstances, and revised at times to honor a teen's growing independence and maturity. Families certainly should not have the same rules for a sixteen-year-old that they have for a six-year-old.

## Have Clear Expectations

We need to share our expectations concerning our children's behavior in our home, at their school, when visiting relatives, and when they are with their friends. In developing or changing the rules, our expectations should be clearly articulated. Teens are skilled at finding the loopholes, so we have to be clear about both the "letter and spirit" of our expectations. Does curfew mean be in the home or just on the property? Who is included in not having anyone in the house while you are out? Does bedtime mean lights out and TV off?

Involving our children in developing family expectations is very valuable. When children have some input, they are more likely to "own" the rules. This involvement is also an opportunity to teach children how to negotiate, compromise, and discuss reasons for rules. Identifying certain benchmarks when expectations can be reviewed and changed is also very important. For instance, on birthdays, school graduations, or other important dates, we might sit down with our children and review the rules and negotiate changes. Curfews, for instance, might be reviewed on one's birthday, or at the beginning of summer. Knowing that the rules change as they get older makes it easier for children to accept and follow the current rules, even when they do not like them.

## Have Logical Consequences

Along with stable rules and clear expectations, we need logical consequences when the rules and expectations are not met. Logical consequences are fair and fit the problem. They are neither excessive nor too lenient. For instance, if our teens come home after curfew, they might lose an equivalent amount of time on their next night out. Grounding them for a week when they are an hour late might be excessive and seem like an overreaction. Ignoring the curfew violation is perhaps too lenient, suggesting that the curfew is not really important.

Again, involving our children in determining the consequences is a very good technique. This assists them in identifying logical consequences. When our teens make a decision leading to negative consequences, let the consequences speak for themselves and let the child live with them. For instance, if our teen chooses to come home late, then they live with the consequences. It is really fair to say, "You made this decision and this is the consequence of your decision." That is better than saying, "You came in late and now

I have to punish you" or "Here's your punishment." To be harsh or authoritarian just fuels further conflict. No parent wants to be in the role of judge, jury, and jailer. If we have clear expectations and logical consequences, then our children have the freedom of making decisions and accepting the consequences. Children can choose to not study or not do homework, and live with the consequences of failed tests or poor grades. They can choose to spend their allowance on something they want, and live with the consequence of not having money for something else. They make decisions and live with the consequences, and we avoid having an emotional fight.

The limit to teens' freedom to make decisions and live with the consequences is when their decision may lead to physical, emotional, or spiritual harm. For instance, we cannot stand by and let our teens make the decision to drink and drive, and then let them live with the consequences, which may include harm to the teen and/or to others. Several of these important issues will be discussed further in this chapter.

### Decide Which Issues Are Important

We do not have to win every fight or battle with our children. When we are willing to give in on an issue, we teach our children how to "win" by saying "you are right about this" and we model how to "lose" gracefully or to compromise, by saying "I am sorry." Every issue is not life or death. So we have to decide which can be used as learning experiences, and which we have to win for the benefit of our children. We should discuss this together with our spouse so that there's a united front when dealing with our children. Some issues where we can let go include:

*Clothes.* This is an area where our children should have choices and be able to make decisions. We will never understand "what is in and what is out" with youth today. And clothes are very important for young people during this period of searching for acceptance from their peers. This does not mean, however, that we should have to buy our children whatever they want and whenever they want

> When we are willing to give in on an issue, we teach our children how to "win" by saying "you are right about this" and we model how to "lose" gracefully or to compromise, by saying "I am sorry."

it. We can make buying clothes an opportunity for teaching our children some basic life skills by giving them a budget for clothing and letting them spend it however they want. They make decisions, consider options, and live with the consequences. And we save our blood pressure. However, we have a responsibility to discuss with our children our standards for modesty, so that parameters are set before we go shopping.

*Their Rooms.* We always have the option of closing the door to our children's room! Controlling the cleanliness of their rooms is an opportunity for our children to live with the consequences of disorderly rooms, piles of dirty clothes, and lost possessions. One technique that is usually effective for getting children to clean their rooms is to encourage them to invite friends for an overnight. Even if this technique does not work, the cleanliness of their room is not a reflection on us, and gives some room for negotiation for the rest of the house: "You can choose to keep your room how you want it, but since we all live in the rest of the house, we have to find an acceptable compromise."

*Music.* Music has always been an avenue for teens' rebellion. Witness the reaction by our parents to Elvis Presley, the Beatles, or the favorite singers when we were teenagers. Certainly, some music today expresses negative values and uses harsh language. But much music also expresses positive values, even if the music is loud and the words seem incomprehensible. Besides, forbidding teens to buy certain types of music is an almost impossible task. They will just listen to the banned albums somewhere else and we will not be around to talk about the values expressed in the lyrics. Rather, when dealing with controversial music, we should listen to the songs with our children and read the words together. Then together discuss the values in the song. Ask, "Is this what you believe about relationships? About love? About sex? About life? Why do you believe this?" At least then we are part of the more important discussion. We can also negotiate limits on the sound volume, so we do not have to listen to the music.

Another important point for us to remember is to never attack the artist, the group, or the type of music, e.g., RAP, heavy metal, alternative, etc. All music has pluses and minuses. We show our children that they are being fair by avoiding generalizations and stereotyping. Keep the discussion on the values expressed in the music: "I am against the values in this song." That way, the discussion centers on values, rather than on how a music group looks and acts. This approach takes some work, but it is worth it—and we can teach our children critical thinking skills. Besides, we do not have to pay for our children's music. Let them pay for their music with their own money. Again, this fosters decision making skills, considering options, and living with consequences.

*Friends.* One of the most difficult and sensitive issues between parents and teenagers is their friends. Youth react strongly to parental criticism about their friends because of the importance of their peer group, an issue described previously. Rather than criticize, we should make an effort to know our children's friends. We should invite them into their home, have snacks and refreshments—a very important sign of hospitality, and talk to them. Spending time enables us to really know our children's friends, while the friends get to know us and our expectations and values. Teens really appreciate their parents' accepting their friends without criticism. Furthermore, since identification with the peer group is so strong, by accepting our children's friends, we are publicly accepting our children. Besides, we can learn much about our teens' interests and values by the values and interests of the friends they choose. So we are encouraged to make our home teen-friendly.

However, several interrelated issues are important for us to "win" and require parents to not compromise because of the potential consequences to our children: parties, drinking, driving, sexual activity, and technology.

*Parties.* Beginning with our children's first invitation to a party or another child's home, we should ask basic questions: Will the parents be home? What is the phone number? How long is the party? When our children are younger, we probably drive them to their parties, giving us the opportunity to introduce ourselves to the host, to clarify pick up times, and also to check out the party. As our children get older, we do less transporting, but our concerns should increase. Will there be parents present? Will they be in the room where the party is being held? Will there be alcohol? We are being fair in asking our teen these questions and also in contacting the party host. Occasionally, the media carries stories about parents allowing drinking at their homes, rationalizing that teens are going to drink anyway and that it is better to drink and stay over night rather than having the teens drive home after drinking. We should be clear that it is unacceptable for other adults to make choices about alcohol and our children. We need to be vigilant about the party issue.

*Drinking.* We have to discuss this issue with our children. We must clearly express our expectations and our reasons. Alcohol is a depressant that inhibits one's ability to make good decisions. Drinking is often an activity that symbolizes moving out of childhood and into young adulthood. We should probably remove the mystery surrounding alcohol, emphasizing that responsible behavior, not drinking itself, is the issue. If alcoholism runs in the family, young people need to know this and the potential physical consequences. Alcohol relates to the following issues.

*Driving.* Receiving one's driving license is an important benchmark of entering young adulthood, and therefore, this is a powerful control. We should be very clear about our expectations concerning driving. Unsafe driving practices by teenagers must carry clear consequences; for instance, paying their own tickets, insurance costs, or repairs. If our teen misses curfew because he or she was driving friends home, then perhaps he or she loses use of the car for a night. We might want to declare drinking and driving a non-negotiable. "If I ever smell alcohol in the car, you will lose your license." These issues need discussion, clear expectations, and logical consequences.

*Sexual Activity.* Sexuality is such a difficult topic for many parents and teens to discuss. Yet, adolescence is marked by an exploding sexual awareness, bombardment by media sexual images, and their searching for intimacy. We have to begin talking with our children about physical development, sexuality, and sexual decision making at appropriate ages. We are being unrealistic if we think that having "the talk" with our children in elementary school or when our teen reaches high school is enough to assist them is dealing with the conflicting messages, feelings, and decisions that surround sexuality. Teens need an opportunity to ask their questions and learn accurate information, especially from us. For many newly sexually active teens, alcohol often plays a role in their decision making—or their inability to make a responsible decision. All of this points to a need for clear communication between us and our teens.

*Technology.* There is no denying the significant impact that technology has on our children today! The Internet, cell phones and their permutations, and MP3 players are an integral and growing part of our lives and we must help our children wisely and safely use technology. The best strategy for protecting our children is educating them about technology and safety and providing clear guidelines for the role of technology in one's life. There are certainly many benefits provided by the Internet today, but there are also critical concerns including safeguarding personal information, handling cyber-issues, avoiding online scams, and being courteous in online communications.

The National Center for Missing and Exploited Children says that allowing our children to go online without supervision or ground rules is like allowing them to explore a major metropolitan area by themselves. The Internet and all technology, like a city, offer an enormous array of entertainment and educational resources, but also present some potential risks. Our children need help navigating this world.

The most effective strategy for protecting young people online is supervision, both high tech and old fashioned. Schools have certainly addressed these issues in their settings. But children now go online almost anywhere. They surf the Internet and send messages from a home computer or one at a friend's home, library, or school. They connect at coffee shops and other hot spots using laptops and wireless connections. Internet-enabled video game systems allow them to compete against and chat with players around the world. Wireless devices enable young people to surf the web and exchange messages, photographs, and short videos from just about anywhere.

It is impossible to watch our children every minute, but we can do more to help them benefit from the Internet and avoid its potential risks. By exploring the Internet with your teens, you greatly expand its capacity as an educational tool. By providing guidance and discussion along the way, you increase teens' online skills and confidence along with their ability to handle cyber-issues.

Each family has to set their standards for acceptable and appropriate behavior and parents are encouraged to negotiate guidelines with their children. These sample guidelines expand on the information provided by the National Center for Missing and Exploited Children.

### The Internet
The Internet does provide the world's largest library, shopping, and entertainment system at one's fingertips. And there is also the potential for sites containing adult images or demeaning, racist, sexist, violent, or false information.

- Choose search engines carefully, some are designed specifically for children and youth. Check with your Internet provider for appropriate filters.
- Help your children find information online. Search the Internet together to help them find reliable sources of information.
- Keep the computer in a central location (e.g., a family room) where supervision is easy.
- Consider parental controls.
- Monitor the sites visited by your teens and ask them about their favorite sites. Go there with them.

### E-Mail
E-Mail is quick and cost effective, transmitting information, messages, documents, and photographs to others in a matter of seconds or minutes. However, teens can often set up accounts through free web-based services without parental permission. E-Mail also exposes our children to spam or phishing which may contain questionable and offensive messages.

- Talk with your children about e-mail accounts and never sharing passwords.
- Check on spam filters.
- Tell your teens to never open e-mails from unknown sources.
- Encourage your teens to report any cyber bullying messages to you and then to appropriate authorities.

## Instant Messaging (IM)

Particularly appealing to young people, IM allows real time communication. IM has its own language, so parents might need a translator.

- Remind your children to IM people they know in real life and to block any sender they do not know.
- Ask your teens to give you a lesson in "IM speak."

## Social Networking

Young people connect with friends and others with similar interests, exchange instant messages, e-mails, photographs, artwork, stories, videos, and music—everything going on in their lives—through social networking sites. However, teens must also understand the dangers and consequences of making details of their private lives available to the public. Whatever is posted is there forever—and that might have serious consequences as young people apply to college or for jobs.

- Help your children create their profile carefully. Does it reflect the kind of person they want to be known as?
- Require that you be added as a "friend" with access to your children's site.
- Be mindful of cyber bullying—the posting of hurtful and mean messages and/or photographs to embarrass a person. Ask your children to talk with you should this happen to them.
- Explicitly discuss what can be posted—because everything posted is permanent.
- Tell your teens not to accept invitations from unknown persons.

## Cell Phones, Wireless Devices, and Texting

Many parents consider cell phones a necessity for their children. It is certainly reassuring to be able to contact our children in an emergency or for important communications. However, cell phones are increasingly used for "sexting"—sending sexually explicit photographs or simply embarrassing photographs that can be posted on the Internet—a form of cyber bullying.

- Create rules about the appropriate use of cell phones and set limits, including with whom your child may communicate and when the cell phone can be used.
- Consider removing the Internet feature or set controls on the cell phone if necessary.

- Remind your children that "sexting" is illegal, immoral, and hurtful. What is posted is now available to everyone forever.
- Determine at what age a child receives a cell phone (e.g., 9th grade after one semester).
- Pick an appropriate text message plan—this is a key way teens communicate.
- Consider time limits; e.g., no cell phone or texting after 10:00 PM.
- Consider use limits; e.g., no cell phones, MP3 players, or texting at school, at the dinner table, at family gatherings, or when there is company.

## Online Gaming

A type of social networking, online private and group gaming connects players through the Internet, creating specific chat rooms, IM functions, text, and gaming communities.

- Keep the gaming console in a common area of the home so you can easily supervise.
- Set rules about how long your child can play, with whom they play, and the type of games.
- Check the rating systems to help you decide which games to allow.

## Resources

There are several excellent websites providing information on technology safety for parents:

- The National Center for Missing and Exploited Children: www.ncmec.org
- Stop Cyber Bullying: www.stopcyberbullying.org
- NetSmartz: www.netsmartz.org
- IKeepSafe.Org: www.ikeepsafe.org

Inevitably, we and our teens will confront other issues. We need to balance where we can afford to let go of control and where we cannot.

## Be Vigilant, But Respect Your Teen's Privacy

Young people have a right to their personal privacy. They have a need for physical privacy in terms of a space to call their own. This is a real challenge in families where bedrooms are shared. Teens have a need for personal space where they can be alone at times. During adolescence some teens begin spending more time alone. They seem more withdrawn, even sullen. They are carving out some space for themselves. Some teens find their privacy in keeping diaries. Even with the best of intentions, reading a child's diary is a major intrusion. This breech of trust is very difficult to mend.

Another way teens establish their space is through language. They answer our questions with one syllable words or grunts. A common parent-teen conversation might sound like this: "Where are you going?" "Out." "What are you going to do?" "Hang out." "When will you be back?" "Later." They are not necessarily being difficult intentionally. They are simply struggling to create some personal boundaries in order to better understand who they are. In order to survive peacefully, families may have to negotiate answering with more than four words. Of course that means that we cannot hide behind "Because I said so" as a reason for our teens to do what they have been told.

Traditionally, teens have their terms and words which create a sense of secrecy and privacy. We should not hesitate to ask what their terms mean. For example, "Going with" as a description for relationships has had different connotations over the past generations. Each generation has had its own terms for various levels of relationships, various groups or types of youth (sports, brains, grunges, nerds, preps, etc.), and for various activities ("let's party" has had various meanings"). We do not need to know the exact definition of everything our teenagers say or mean, but when necessary, we should ask for a clarification or meaning and not assume we know what our children are talking about.

Another means of teenagers carving out their individual space is through their conversations with us—or lack thereof. Sometimes we will find that our children have become less open and willing to share about school, their friends, or their activities. Withdrawing from conversation or withholding information and becoming more secretive may be a way for our teens to establish their identity. Information is power, and controlling how much we know about them, their friends, and their activities is a way for our teens to experience personal power. However, a sudden turn to total secrecy may be a sign that a teen is engaging in behavior that might upset us. Even though privacy is important, we should still be aware of what our teens are doing, with whom they are associating, and where they are spending time or hanging out. Through genuinely interested questions, time spent together, having their friends in the house, attending parent-teacher meetings at school, and involvement in their other activities where appropriate, we can have a good sense of what is happening in the lives of our children.

### Respect Their Individuality

This struggle to carve out a space for themselves is a reminder for us to be especially attentive to our teens as individuals. Teens need to feel accepted as themselves. They need to be appreciated as unique persons who are developing their own sense of values, beliefs, goals, and interests. Even when the changes are not necessarily noticeable, we have to remember the internal explosions that are happening. The changes are there and it is both wonderful and frightening. The changes are wonderful in that the child is becoming his or her own person, taking more responsibility for his or her life. And that is also frightening. The teen is now caught between the security and comfort of home and family and the fascination of their peer group and the rest of their world.

We need to respect our teens as individuals, with their new experiences, concerns, dreams, and desires. We have to remember that, despite the fact that adolescence has been happening for quite a while, this is the first time for this child. And our teen might experiment with a different persona, as expressed in his or her clothes, music, activities, language, and friends. During this time, our teen may become someone we do not like, someone who is different from the person we expected him or her to become. We have to be careful of the conscious and unconscious expectations that we have for our children, because this is a time when our teens may disappoint us, especially when they appear to be someone other than our ideal image of what teens should be. We need to remember that this time of growth and experimentation is important in order for them to develop their sense of individuality. Perhaps we need to hang up the poster with the saying, "Be patient. God is not finished with me yet." This poster may have been designed for teenagers for they really are works in progress. We can draw some solace and comfort from the adage, "The fruit does not fall far from the tree." In the long term, our children will pick up most of our values, though lived out in their unique manner.

In families with more than one child moving through adolescence, it is especially important for us to pay attention to each of our children specifically. Traditions like taking the child out to breakfast or dinner on his or her birthday, or allowing him or her to choose their own birthday dinner at home, or occasional outings with the individual child are ways of acknowledging his or her special importance. Children are simultaneously members of the family and individuals and they need to be treated as both. Indeed, guarding teens' individuality while fostering their sense of belonging is a balancing act for parents, but one filled with rewards.

## Waste Time with Your Teens

In the desire to develop a meaningful and loving relationship with our children while fulfilling all our commitments and responsibilities as adults, we often try to carve out opportunities for "quality time" with our children. At times, this desperate attempt leads to an overabundance of organized activities. We begin equating our success as parents with the number of clubs, sports, and activities in which our children participate. We fall into the "chauffeur" style of parenting, living by our calendar of commitments and driving responsibilities. Sometimes both we and our children forget for whose benefit all of this activity is planned. This lifestyle may also blind us to a basic value: It is the time we waste on our children that makes our children feel important.

Wasting time is especially challenging, and seems almost sinful, in a society that values time for what can be accomplished or produced within its confines. But genuine conversation happens best during the less stressed, less structured, free time. Without the pressure of an agenda or schedule, more serious questions and concerns arise. During these times bonds of trust and genuine communication are created. Sharing opinions about school, community, church, national, and global issues and listening to children's views is a very important expression of respect. We are signaling that our teens have opinions that are worth listening to, especially if we do not necessarily agree with those opinions. But remember, teens will often take a view that is contrary to our view just as a means of establishing a sense of independence. So relax, listen, and ask for their opinions. And waste time, for the benefit of the entire family.

*Love Your Teens Unconditionally*

Sometimes, young people get the message that love is earned, that being loved is based on getting good grades, making the sports team, going to the right school, or having the right friends. Being loved is tied into being accepted and being accepted is integral to one's self-esteem. But this is conditional love. Conditional love is probably the greatest source of stress for children for they find themselves constantly trying to live up to artificial criteria in order to be loved.

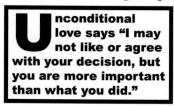

Unconditional love is a free gift. Persons are loved because of who they are, not because of what they do, what they own, or what they accomplish. Our children need our unconditional love. We need to tell our children, and our teenagers, that we love them. Do not assume they know they are loved. During the explosions of adolescence very little, if anything, is certain for teenagers. They need to hear they are loved, loved for who they are. We need to love our children like we did when we had more control over them. Children never outgrow their need for love, though they do outgrow their need for control.

We have to also remember that our children love us, even if they have difficulty expressing this love. Believing in unexpressed love is perhaps the most difficult when our children or teens make a decision that has painful consequences. What is the most appropriate reaction if a teen became pregnant, or was arrested, or engaged in some other negative behavior? Unconditional love says "I may not like or agree with your decision, but you are more important than what you did." This does not imply that consequences are avoided or downplayed. However, the parental task is to love our children unconditionally and intentionally.

*Tell Your Children That They Are Doing a Good Job*

Affirmation is very important. Sometimes teenagers just need to hear that they are doing okay. In their struggle to establish their own identity, to be part of the family even as they pull away, and to negotiate the ups and downs of adolescence, it is very easy for teens to be highly self-critical. They find it easier to name their faults than their strengths and to identify their shortcomings rather than their accomplishments. We should, for no special reason, just let our teens know that they are doing a fine job of growing up. A popular adage states that in order to make it in life, every one needs just one person who is absolutely sold on them. We should be that person for our children. Tell them: "I am absolutely sold on you," "You are doing a good job of growing up," "You have become a wonderful teenager," "I am proud of you." Of course, this does not prevent the next round of conflicts, issues, and confrontations. But affirmation does create an atmosphere where the tensions can be handled and love is not forgotten.

We need to balance affirmation or the positive reinforcement of our children and the inevitable criticism of teens' inappropriate behavior. A good rule of thumb is to provide four affirmations or positive strokes for every critique or negative comment. If we really want our children to listen to a critique of their behavior, the critique must be balanced with affirmations, though not at the same time. This balance of affirmation and critique is true especially for teenagers because their self-esteem takes such a beating during the explosions of adolescence. Teens often believe that they only hear from adults when they have made a mistake.

A common complaint that teenagers have of us is that the only time we pay any attention to them is when they have done something wrong. As one teen said to me during a phone call in which she painfully shared her desire to commit suicide, "I hate my parents. They never say anything when I do well in school or if I do my chores. But just let me mess up once and they are in my face. They only pay attention to me when I do something wrong. But sometimes, negative attention is better than no attention at all." Children of all ages hunger for attention and the affirmation that they are okay.

Finding at least four opportunities to compliment teens can be challenging. But if we want to avoid becoming solely the bearer of bad news and if we want our children to take our critique seriously, then we have to also affirm the behaviors, the decisions, and even the attitudes that are positive. In fact, by complimenting our children, we are actually affirming the behavior we want them to exhibit. For instance, when we say, "I appreciate the way you helped clear the dinner table (or did your homework, finished your chores, talked with your grandparents, etc.)," we are identifying the behaviors we value. Positive affirmations reinforce behavior, because everyone likes compliments. So we should look for opportunities to honestly praise the specific behaviors and actions that we desire in our children. Remember: "You are doing a good job of growing up. You are becoming so mature and self-reliant. I am really proud of you." A practical skill for effectively affirming children will be more fully described in the next chapter.

### The Greater Burden Is on the Adult

Given the natural generation gap that developmentally exists between parents and their adolescent children, the greater burden of responsibility to bridge this gap is on us. After all, we have more experience, more maturity, and more insight, if not more patience. This does not lessen the responsibility of teens to work at bridging the gap, but it is not a 50/50 proposition. We have to be willing to take the first step. That may mean offering reconciliation, or saying "I am sorry," "I miss sharing with you," "I miss talking to you," or "Can we talk?" We have to model forgiveness, genuine listening, and effective communication. We model what it means to be in relationship.

Our own adolescent years serve as a reminder that teenagers change, parents change, and their relationship will change. In families where there is much verbal, emotional, and perhaps even physical pain, some parents feel rejected or that they have failed and they are tempted to burn their bridges and end their relationship with their teens. These parents, especially, have to keep perspective and take the long view about their relationships with their children.

Adolescence is a time of testing and pushing against parental and other limits. It is a time of questioning and challenging. The challenge is to keep perspective, be patient, and remember that children who navigate adolescence with their parents' support and love become the young adults who support and love their parents.

# Chapter 4

## *Self-Esteem: Making Champions of Our Children*

Self-Esteem is a concept that is receiving much attention in education, family, and societal arenas today. Everyone seems concerned about how children and youth feel about themselves, recognizing the impact that self-esteem has on how one perceives his or her own value, abilities, and sense of the future. However, self-esteem is not an easy concept to define. For the purposes of this chapter, self-esteem is understood as a belief in oneself, a sense of self-worth and self-respect that comes from thoughts, feelings, sensations, and experiences. Self-Esteem reflects the extent to which persons believe they are capable, significant, and successful.

A child's self-esteem is influenced by many factors: parents and family, school environment, peer group, church involvement, community involvement, and other significant adults. Self-Esteem is reflected in one's values, educational aspirations, positive view of the future, ability to make friends, ability to make good decisions, school performance, willingness to try new experiences, and in one's faith life.

### Loveable and Capable

Perhaps the most succinct definition of self-esteem lies in the title of a short, elaborately illustrated parable from my youth, "I Am Loveable and Capable." In the story a boy, whose name I have long forgotten, gets up in the morning and puts on his IALAC sign (I am loveable and capable). The story follows the boy through his day at school, filled with a variety of positive and negative experiences affecting his IALAC sign. With each of those experiences which lessen his self-esteem, such as losing his homework, having a car splash mud on his clothes, getting hassled by a group of older bullies, being yelled at by his parents for coming home late, a piece of his IALAC sign is torn off. For each positive experience, such as a teacher's compliment, correctly answering a question in school, having a female classmate say hello, a piece of his sign is added on. On this particular day, the negatives outweigh the positives, so that when he finally goes to bed, his IALAC sign is the size of a postage stamp.

Every child wears an "IALAC sign. Some signs are more resilient than others, some are more durable, and some are steadily disappearing. The IALAC sign is a useful image to describe the impact that parents and all who interact with children and youth have on their self-esteem.

Two very important components are included in the IALAC concept: loveable and capable. Children and youth need to know they are loveable because of who they are, without requirements. Unconditional acceptance and love means that parents place no conditions on their love for their children and teenagers. Unconditional love does not mean that parents always love what their children do, but unconditional love does challenge parents to separate their reaction to the behavior from their feelings for the person. We may not like the action or behavior, e.g., breaking curfew, failing a school subject, or even drinking or trying drugs, but we need to be clear that our love is not based on what our children do, but on who our children are as our sons and daughters.

Unconditional love also says love is not based on the good things our children do. For example, we should not give our children the message that we love them because they get good grades, make the sports team, or do their chores. The trap in giving this message is that if our children fail a course, get cut from a team, or forget their chores, they may think that we no longer love them. Our children may see our love as based on their accomplishments, and that is very conditional.

With their peers this conditional acceptance is even more serious. Often, teenagers think their acceptance by their peers is based on what they own, how they dress, who they date, or where they live; very conditional acceptance. But given the power of the peer group when young people begin to pull away from their parents and family, this conditional acceptance is very powerful nonetheless.

So an important task for all parents is convincing their children that they are loveable. And, as discussed in the previous chapter, to love them means to set boundaries and limits. Rarely, however, do our children understand that setting limits and rules is a reflection of our parental love. Even as we strive to love our children for whom they are, our children may not seem to even like us in return. However, at this stage of development, being respected may be more important for us than being loved by our children. So good parents love their children, they tell their children that they love them, and they act like they love them, in some way convincing them that they are loveable.

But . . . young people need more than outside affirmation and love. Because adolescents are in this stage of physical, emotional, values, and relational explosions, affirmation has to be connected to adolescents' experience of themselves, if the affirmation is to be seen as authentic. Our teens may unconsciously believe that we have to love them because we are their parents. Parental affirmation may seem meaningless and empty if a child does not believe or accept that affirmation, if a child feels unlovable. For affirmation and love to be experienced as authentic by children and teenagers, this affirmation has to be connected to the second characteristic of IALAC—capable. Affirmation seems more genuine when the words of affirmation are connected to youths' experience of themselves as able to do things.

## Life Skills
This understanding of "capable" is different from success at sports and school. "Capable" in terms of self-esteem is rooted in competence and confidence, rooted in children's ability to handle basic life skills. Capable means having mastery of the basic life skills that are needed to simply survive and interact in a complex society. Life skills include their ability to form various types of relationships, to develop plans of action, and to handle the natural stress and anxiety caused by life. So, life skills include the ability to make friends, to handle a job, to follow directions, set goals, solve problems, make good decisions, respond to others' needs, accept and give forgiveness, manage their time, listen to others, express

> "Capable" in terms of self-esteem is rooted in competence and confidence, rooted in children's ability to handle basic life skills.

oneself, communicate with others, resolve conflicts, be sensitive to others, handle social situations, manage stress, and so on. Perhaps we have taken these skills for granted, because after all, as we were growing up, learning these skills probably just happened. We probably were not even aware of learning these skills. Yet, today, many young people have not learned these basic life skills, and that negatively impacts their self-esteem.

Exercise #10, "Making Good Decisions: The DECIDE Approach" provides a clear outline that you and your teen can use together when dealing with a decision. In so doing, you will be helping your teen learn a valuable and essential life skill.

In the past, learning these skills was less complex because guidelines for behavior were more clearly and constantly supported by group norms, i.e., the neighborhood, school, and church. But in a changing society, and given the impact of television and other media, young people today are confronted with a variety of value systems, belief systems, behaviors, and environments, and often without regard for fostering positive behaviors. Watching how television handles conflict resolution where the biggest gun always seems to win, or depicts relationships and commitment where touch and go relationships seem to be the norm are examples of how important life skills are not reinforced in the medium that impacts young people.

There is a need to affirm children's and teen's capabilities specifically, identifying the behavior that we like and the reasons we like it. An important parenting skill is the ability to identify and affirm good behaviors. Parents have only two ways to change children's behaviors: to reinforce the good and correct the bad. When we manage children's behavior by reinforcing the good, we are acknowledging a skill or competence and that makes the behavior or life skill repeatable.

For instance: when parents tell their child, "You did a nice job of cleaning up your room. Your clothes are put away, your school books are stacked neatly, and your bed is made. I am pleased because now your room will look nice for company," not only have parents affirmed their children's skill of cleaning their room, but they have also identified the elements of that skill, and they have given a reason for using that skill. The skill of cleaning one's room includes the elements of putting clothes away, stacking books, and making the bed. The parents have taught the skill of cleaning the room, reinforced the behavior, and affirmed the child's sense of feeling capable. And the parents have given their child a reason for using this skill, other than "I said so!"

Another example with a teenager: "Thanks very much for calling us and telling us you were going to be late. We really worry about you when you are late, so we appreciated knowing where you were and when you would be home." Teen responsibility includes informing parents when they will be late, and the parents have identified the reasons why they want to know about late arrivals home. This is much more effective than, "Just wait until you get home, if you cannot handle the curfew then you are grounded." Now, that does not mean that there are not times when there have to be consequences for behaviors, which will be described later.

So, in terms of self-esteem, young people need to feel loveable and capable. Children and youth need to be affirmed for whom they are and they need to have their basic life competencies identified and affirmed. When we identify our children's skills and gifts, we contribute to our children's experience of uniqueness and specialness. When young people are able to use their life skills in situations which require those skills, their sense of personal self-confidence is fostered. Feeling capable enhances their self-esteem.

You will notice in the above examples that life skills are all identifiable behaviors. A life skill is observable. Exercise #8, "Trustworthiness," uses six identifiable behaviors to measure the level of trust and trustworthiness in your parent-teen relationship. Although we all have three capabilities—thinking, feeling, and behavior—only behavior can be seen. When a person changes the way he or she is thinking or feeling that is an internal change and may not be observable to anyone else. We really do not know what a person is thinking or feeling—unless it is experienced in behavior. A change in behavior is an external change, and it is measurable, observable, and identifiable. Since childrens' and teens' sense of being capable is rooted in their behavior, we want to teach behaviors that will enable them to feel confident and competent in life situations. We are much more likely to act our way into a new way of thinking than we are to think our way into a new way of acting. By teaching new ways of acting, and new life skills, we will be affecting our children's way of thinking and believing about themselves.

For example, when a child says, "Why do I have to go to Mass on Sunday?" this is a teaching discussion, not a theological discussion. "You are going to Mass because someday you will need faith." Later, we can talk with him or her about God, faith, and prayer, but right now, going to Mass is the behavior, the life skill that we want. "Why do I have to go to grandmom's house?" "Because spending time with family is important to us." Family involvement is the behavior, the life skill we want.

## Practical Strategies for Developing Life Skills

Father Flanagan's Boys Town community has researched strategies that are effective in fostering life skills in children

and young people. Three such strategies have been described which we can use to reinforce positive behaviors and also teach new life skills. These strategies do not replace parenting; rather they are incorporated into our current parenting style. Good parents probably already use these or similar approaches unconsciously, but a careful description of these three strategies: effective praise, preventive teaching, and corrective teaching, can be very beneficial.

### Effective Praise

This technique encourages and reinforces positive behavior by identifying the component elements of a positive behavior or life skill. Listen to the difference between these two praise statements.

"Shannon, thank you for paying attention to me while I have been talking to you."

"Shannon, thank you for paying attention to me while I have been talking to you. You have looked me in the eyes, nodded your head, and even smiled once when I was talking. It shows me that you have been listening and I appreciate that."

Obviously, the second praise statement not only affirms the behavior, but identifies the elements of the behavior. If a child does not really know what "paying attention" means, then this praise statement reinforces the behavior, while teaching the skill. This example is similar to the "child cleaning his or her room" and the "teen calling because he or she is going to be late for curfew" examples previously used. Praise is more effective when we can identify the elements of the skill or behavior, and the reason this skill is good to have. Effective praise includes three components:

- Show approval of the behavior
- Identify the elements of the behavior
- Give a reason why the behavior is important

Imagine what effective praise would sound like in the following situations:

- Your teen finishes a school project on time (or early!).

  "Nice job in completing your school project. You really planned well, stuck to your priorities, and managed your time. That is a real sign of taking responsibility."

- Your teen decides not to go a party which had you worried.

  "I think you made a very good decision and I know it was not easy for you. But you weighed all the possible consequences and chose what was best for you. That takes a degree of real maturity."

- Your teen gets up for school independently of your efforts.

  "Nice job of getting up on your own. You picked the right time for you, set the clock, and got everything done in time for school. You really are taking more control over your life and you make mornings easier for me."

Chapter 3 stressed the importance of a 4 to 1 ratio of affirming our children to critiques. Utilizing "effective praise" enables us to do so.

A subtle use of effective praise concerns the third step in the technique. When possible, we should give reasons for the behavior that impact other people. For instance, when children listen, not only will they hear what is being said, but they also make the speaker feel good. When a teen makes a good decision, not only is the teen acting more responsible, but the parents feel better about how their child is maturing. When our children are quiet at the movie theater, not only can they hear the movie, but the rest of the audience can hear also. We can begin at their early ages teaching our children to act in particular ways because of how their behavior affects other people. In teaching "other-centered" rationales for doing the behavior, we are introducing our children to moral behavior and moral thinking.

### Preventive Teaching

This skill identifies a necessary behavior or skill by describing the elements of the skill and the reason the skill or behavior is desired. This technique teaches the necessary skill prior to the skill actually being needed. Doing so fosters a sense of confidence in a child or teen because the youngster will know how to act in a particular situation. For example:

> "Shannon, when your grandparents are visiting, could you please be polite and sociable, by entering into conversation, listening to them while they are speaking, and staying at the dinner table until dinner is completely finished. That way your grandparents will know that you care about them. Does that make sense to you? Can I see that "I'm interested" look you have? Thanks, I really appreciate your willingness to hang out with your grandparents."

Preventive teaching includes five components:

- Describe the behavior that is desired.
- Give a reason why the behavior is important.
- Have them acknowledge what you are saying.
- Practice the behavior, if appropriate.
- Praise and affirm them.

Imagine what preventive teaching would sound like in the following situations:

- Preparing your teen for driving with other teens.

"Andy, soon you will be driving with your friends in the car. Can we agree on some basic ground rules, such as: you will always drive safely and there will never be anyone in the car who has been drinking? If someone has been drinking, even if they are a close friend of yours, they may do something that interferes with your driving and possibly cause an accident. And if someone is injured while you are driving; I think you would feel terrible. Does that make sense? If you are not sure how to avoid a situation, I would rather you call me and we will figure out a plan. Okay? Thanks, Andy, I feel confident about your driving."

- Preparing your teen for going out to parties where drinking might occur.

"Regina, now that you are starting to go to parties, I think we need to discuss handling parties where alcohol might be present. I hope you will have the strength to resist the temptation by saying something like, 'No thanks, I do not like beer,' or 'No thanks, I am still drinking this Coke.' Have you thought about how you will handle someone offering you something to drink? What would you say? Can we practice your 'favorite line?' And you can always call me if things are getting out of control. I just have a real fear about parties and alcohol. Does my concern make sense? Thanks, Regina, I feel good about your handling tough situations."

- Preparing your teen for handling dating situations which could get physically out of control.

"Shannon, have you thought about how you would handle a date that was acting physically inappropriate toward you? I worry about you finding yourself in a situation that you cannot control. Perhaps saying something like 'You are making me feel very uncomfortable' or 'I'm not at all ready for this' or 'You have crossed the boundary and I want to go home' would be helpful. Do you have any ideas? Can we practice your favorite line? I have a real fear about possible tough situations and I do not want to see you get hurt or feel scared. Do you understand my concern? Thanks, Shannon. I think you will handle this well."

Using this technique also provides us an opportunity to discuss our expectations with our children, while providing them with the skill to fulfill the expectation. Much frustration and even conflict can be caused when children and youth do not know how to carry out their parents' expectations, even if they want to comply.

> **C**orrective teaching is used to stop a problem behavior, give a consequence, and describe the behavior or skill that is desired.

### Corrective Teaching

This skill helps us respond when our teens do something we do not like. Corrective teaching is used to stop a problem behavior, give a consequence, and describe the behavior or skill that is desired. The important component in this technique is replacing the problem behavior with a desired behavior, which is more effective than just stopping a negative action. For example:

> "Shannon, I need you to stop walking away from me when I am talking to you. If you cannot listen now, then you will have to come in an hour early tonight and we will talk then. I realize you are upset, but rather than walk away from me, it is better to just stay and try to talk this problem out. Does that make any sense to you? Can we try to talk with each other? I would really appreciate talking this through. Thank you for your willingness to try talking this out."

Corrective teaching includes six components:

- Stop the problem behavior.
- Give a consequence for the problem behavior.
- Describe the desired behavior.
- Have them acknowledge what you are saying.
- Practice the desired behavior, if feasible.
- Praise and affirm them.

Imagine what corrective teaching would sound like in the following situations:

- Your teen comes home after curfew without calling you.
- Your teen has alcohol on his or her breath.
- Your teen is fighting with his or her siblings.

In corrective teaching, we should not get caught up in the content of an issue—the reasons, explanations, and excuses. That is almost always an impossible quagmire. We should go right to the behavior that we want to change and the behavior we want to foster. Imagine what corrective teaching would sound like in the following situations:

- Your teen comes home after curfew without calling you.

  "Brian, I thought we agreed that you would call if you were going to be late. Since you were an hour late coming in, your curfew will be an hour earlier for next week. I really need you to call if you are going to be late, because I worry if I do not know where you are. Do you understand how I feel about this? Okay. Thanks for talking this through."

- Your teen has alcohol on his or her breath.

  "Maggie, I smell alcohol on your breath. We will have to talk more about this tomorrow morning, but know that you will be grounded. I feel very strongly about teenagers and drinking and I do not accept your drinking. We have talked about ways of avoiding drinking, and we will talk more about this tomorrow. Do you understand my concerns about this? Okay. Thanks for listening and we will talk tomorrow."

- Your teen is fighting with his or her siblings.

  "Jeff, stop fighting with your brother right now. I think you need to spend some time in your room. If your brother is bothering you, let me handle it, or remove yourself from the situation. You do not have to get into a fight with someone who is much younger than you. Do you understand what I am saying? Does it make any sense? Now, I appreciate you listening to me. I will see you in an hour. And as for you . . . (younger brother) . . ."

Corrective teaching is a complex parenting skill because it includes stopping an undesirable behavior and replacing that behavior with a more appropriate behavior. Often, this skill is utilized in situations that involve a form of conflict, where tension is present.

These examples may sound stilted and artificial and hardly like real life. That is because the emotion is not well portrayed. Therefore, two important points need to be mentioned. First, when emotions are running high, we should call time out before dealing with the problem. For example, waiting until morning to deal with curfew violations or drinking problems may be a better approach than confronting the issue late at night. Calling time out allows the emotions to calm down and also gives us time to think through what we want to say and any possible consequences which may be warranted. Second, these skills need practice. At first, we will stumble through these strategies, but with practice, they will become second nature.

## Some Final Suggestions

The following is a list of practical suggestions for enhancing self-esteem, related to the suggestions for practical parenting in the previous chapter.

1.  Call your child or teen by name.
2.  Use effective praise (4 to 1 ratio), identifying your children's skills.
3.  Teach your children life skills.
4.  Listen to your children, looking into their eyes.
5.  Comfort them when they need comforting.
6.  Ask for and respect their opinions.
7.  Accept your children as they are right now.
8.  Provide an orderly and stimulating environment.
9.  Provide activities that neither bore nor frustrate them.
10. Give them an appropriate level of responsibility.
11. Use positive forms of discipline, practicing corrective teaching.
12. Be consistent.
13. Set reasonable limits on their behavior and explain your expectations. With teenagers, these can be set through mutual discussion.
14. Give your children some control by providing choices.
15. Make promises and follow through.
16. Spend time doing things together.
17. Help your children learn how to get along in a group.

A final reminder: these strategies enable parents to reinforce positive behaviors, identify new behaviors or skills desired, and to confront negative behaviors and replace them with a more appropriate behavior. Having command of desired behaviors or skills, and knowing when to use them, fosters a child's or teen's sense of being capable. When parents use these skills in a spirit of care and love, they affirm their children's sense of being loveable. I Am Loveable and Capable is at the heart of self-esteem.

# Chapter 5

## *Fostering Teens' Faith: Roots and Wings*

One of the more challenging parental tasks today is passing on faith beliefs and convictions to children. Contrary to when most of us grew up, in today's society faith is an option, not a given. As a child growing up in a Catholic family, I do not remember having any choices about church participation. Going to Mass and attending Catholic schools was a given for me. It is what our family did and I was a willing participant. Not until college did I experience any genuine options concerning religion. Even then, as I searched through my faith and understanding of God, I attended a Catholic college so I was still immersed in the Catholic environment. That upbringing has been a wonderful blessing for me and I suspect that many adults have had a similar experience.

Today, however, regardless of where children go to school, attend religious education programs, or participate in the life of the church, they are faced with multiple options concerning religion, values, and belief systems. Also, children cannot be nor should be "programmed" for faith and religious practice. Faith is ultimately a free response to God's grace, and no one can be forced into that response. That does not mean, though, that parents have no impact on their children's faith. In fact, parents are the primary influence in the faith development of their children.

This chapter will describe the process of faith development in order to better understand our teenagers' struggle with religion and church, and will also provide some practical strategies for fostering teens' maturing in faith.

### Process of Faith Development

This phrase indicates that faith develops in individuals in much the same way as one matures psychologically, personally, emotionally, and physically. Faith is a process of growth in relationship with God and God's people and continues to grow and mature throughout one's life. However, distinguishing between our relationship with God and our relationship with the community of believers is important. This relationship with the community—the church—is better understood as religion. Religion is the public expression of our relationship with God, which can be understood as faith. Faith is our personal relationship with God, while religion is our relationship with the community of believers. This distinction is important for understanding the faith maturing process in adolescents.

A useful image for understanding this distinction is a person's name. Everyone has a first and last name and each says something different. First names identify persons as unique individuals with our own characteristics, qualities, hopes, dreams, strengths, and weaknesses. First names are signs of our individuality. Faith is similar to first names. Faith is the unique and individual relationship that we have with God. In the Scriptures there are many examples of God calling people by name, and even changing their first name as a sign of that special calling. Abram becomes Abraham, Simon becomes Peter, Saul becomes Paul, and so on. Faith is a person's first name when it comes to relating with God.

We also have a last name, which denotes our belonging to a family. Families have shared looks, mannerisms, experiences, stories, history, and ways of celebrating. All members are connected in the family, even as they maintain their identity as individuals. Religion is the last name of our faith identity. Religion is the family of faith name. I am a Catholic Christian. I belong to the Catholic family, sharing in the traditions, history, creed, rituals, and beliefs of the Catholic community. Our religious denomination or worshipping community is our last name of faith. This image of having a first and last name is helpful in understanding the process of faith development in adolescents.

### Three Dimensions of Faith
Faith has three important dimensions: believing, trusting, and doing. Faith is often equated with what a person believes about God, or with one's personal relationship of trust in God, or even with how a person acts because of one's beliefs about and relationship with God. Indeed, faith is all three.

Faith as believing relates to our cognitive or intellectual capacity. This dimension is the "what" or content of faith: the creeds, traditions, and beliefs of faith as found in church teachings, prayers, and for Roman Catholics, in the *Catechism of the Catholic Church*. Faith as trusting points toward a personal relationship with a God who cares for and watches over each of us. This is the affective dimension of faith anchored in our feeling personally close to God who is seen as acting within our life. Finally, faith also has a behavioral dimension in that all people are challenged to live out what they believe about their relationship with God. Faith as doing God's will includes participation in the worship and activities of the church community, as well as having a compassionate outreach to our neighbors in every arena of a person's life.

## Styles of Faith

So, how do teens experience and express faith—believing, trusting, and doing—and how does that change throughout their developmental process? Looking back at chapter 2 concerning the developmental tasks during adolescence, parents will find parallels in the faith development of young people. Adolescence was described as a time of testing, questioning, and challenging parents and other authority in order to develop a sense of independence and individuality. Religion is not immune to this process.

Based on the work and scholarship of John Westerhoff, four styles of faith can be described. Westerhoff uses the word "styles," not "stages," in order to avoid seeming judgmental or implying that one stage is better or more mature than another. Westerhoff uses the image of a tree in order to understand how faith develops, each style represented by a ring of the tree.

### Experienced Faith

With the person at the center of the rings, the first style of faith is "experienced faith." Experienced faith is the faith of infants and children. During these early years faith is first experienced primarily through interaction with other "faithing individuals." In experiencing love through their parents, children come to understand that God loves them. In experiencing kindness, forgiveness, security, and acceptance through their parents, children come to understand God as a God who is interested in them personally. For children at this age, parents are the most important people in their lives. Children's image of God is commensurate with their image of their parents.

This style is also characterized by children's imitating their parents' behavior, not because they understand it, but because they believe it is important since their parents see it as important. Children will imitate the actions and attitude of their parents in both family and church rituals. Church even has a magical sense, with the stories, prayers, and rituals taking on a special quality for children. In experienced faith, children's experience of trust, love, and acceptance are critical for developing a sense of faith.

*Affiliative Faith*
During later childhood and into early adolescence the individual moves into the second style of faith, "affiliative faith." Affiliative faith, as the name implies, is characterized by a sense of belonging. Having experienced a sense of affiliation at home, children and youth now want to join clubs, organizations, and teams. They have a need to belong to church as well. The community of believers provides an identity for our children, their "last name of faith" or their religion. Our children have a need to hear the stories and traditions of this family of faith, they want to participate in the rituals, and they want to act with other members of the faith community. In short, children and youth want to do all the things that other members do. Younger adolescents are copiers. They copy the behaviors, dress, and beliefs of those they admire. They want to belong, reflecting the hunger described in chapter one. These feelings of belonging and affiliation characterize this style as "religion of the heart." This sense of belonging will become part of their "roots."

*Searching Faith*
During older adolescence and perhaps into young adulthood, young people developmentally are asserting their individuality. They begin pushing against their parents' rules and limits, questioning everything they once accepted. They are developing their "wings." This pushing and questioning is certainly true also of this "searching style" of faith. If you have ever faced the question "Why do I have to go to church?" you have experienced this style of faith in your children.

Older teens are searching for meaning in life, they hunger for meaning and purpose, and for values they can call their own, and they are testing what they have been taught. Doubt and critical judgment are necessary during this "religion of the head," for they need to test the community's story and understanding of faith in order to reach convictions of their own. During this time of growth, teens are developing their "first name of faith," their personal understanding and relationship with God. At times teens may seem to have lost their faith because they question their religion's beliefs, rituals, and traditions. A more accurate understanding is to say that in some real sense teens are losing their "religion," even while they are developing their own "faith." In reality, religion is not necessarily lost, as much as placed on the back burner, as teens move from a community understanding of faith to a more personal understanding of faith. Teens often say that they pray best in their own rooms, listening to music, or while walking in the woods or along a beach. Often times, they experience God more personally in creation, than they do in a church with other, mostly adult, people.

> Older teens are searching for meaning in life, they hunger for meaning and purpose, and for values they can call their own, and they are testing what they have been taught.

During this time of development, just as in their psychological development, teens often pull away from their parents in order to experience a degree of independence. The presence of other caring trusted adults and young adults in teens' lives who can answer their questions, challenge their reasoning, and provide stability is especially important. This point will be further described in the practical strategies.

### Owned Faith

The good news is that when navigated effectively, the searching style of faith leads into "owned faith." Owned faith is the culmination of the process which has been traditionally called conversion and characterized by strength of conviction and belief. From a religion of the heart to one of the head and now to "religion of the will," the young adult or adult now has developed a religion that they can call their own, a faith that can be put into action. They struggle to eliminate the gap between belief and actions by committing themselves to a lifestyle in which they really do what they believe. This is a major change in a person's thinking, feeling, willing, and acting. In owned faith, the person's first name and last name of faith are now freely chosen. Faith and religion now make sense, provide meaning and direction, and are deserving of a personal commitment to both God and the community of believers.

A word of caution about the interrelationship of the various styles of faith, however, is necessary. Returning to Westerhoff's image of the tree for depicting the growth in faith, we have to remember that trees do not leave their rings behind as they grow. Likewise in faith development, when a young person seems to be in the searching style of faith, parents cannot forget that they still need the experience of faith and the sense of belonging provided by the earlier styles. And owned faith does not mean that teens (or parents) will not have any more questions. Rather, questioning is the means to further growth in faith, coming to ever deeper understandings of God and the challenge of belonging to a community of believers. The styles are simply a way to better understand faith as a journey throughout one's life, rather than a particular destination. One style is not better or more advanced than another. They overlap, compliment each other, and help name the experience of faith one has.

## Principles and Strategies
Throughout this journey of faith, there are practical strategies and experiences that we can utilize to foster this faith maturing process in our children and teens.

### Practice Our Religion
The number one influence on the faith of young people is the faith life of their parents. Recent research on teenagers finds that the

faith beliefs and practices of adolescents actually mirror the faith beliefs and practices of their parents. So the way we practice our religion had great impact on our children. Our participation in Sunday Mass or worship and our involvement in the life of the parish church by participating in retreats, Bible study groups, church organizations and ministries, or adult catechesis sessions are signs to our children that our religion is a significant part of our lives. Parental church involvement grows out of the affiliative style of faith and nurtures parental owned faith. Participation in the church reminds our child that belonging to a community of believers is integral to sustaining and expressing faith.

*Model Our Faith*
In addition to belonging to a worshipping community, we have a great impact on our children's faith when we live our faith in our daily routines and interactions. Faith should influence our lifestyle choices, use of time, how we handle conflicts, the relationships we form, and even how we handle work issues. Perhaps the two most obvious challenges to the impact of faith in real life are how adults drive their car and act at sports events! Do we pray at home in the evening? before family meals? in restaurants? In our prayers do we remember those less fortunate? Do we pray for our teens' intentions? For their friends? Do we model forgiveness and reconciliation in our lives by admitting when we are wrong and not lording it over someone else who has been wrong? How do we handle crises in our life, such as death, divorce, pregnancy, illness? Does our faith impact how we celebrate Christmas, Easter, or other holy days? All of these situations are part of life. Young people watch to see if our faith makes sense to us, if faith works for us. Youth are looking for a faith that provides meaning in all areas of their life, and not just on Sundays.

*Talk About Values*
Faith has to influence our values. When young people start asking the "why" questions, we should be prepared to answer through the lens of our values and our faith. "Why can I not go drinking? Why should I take school seriously? Why should I abstain from sexual relationships?" These questions, along with the issues of racism and prejudice, justice for others, and a comprehensive approach to life, are opportunities for parents to express their values, anchoring them in their faith beliefs. Though the temptation is to answer, "Because I said so!" young people really need to hear

how we have come to a decision and what values influence our decision making process. By sharing our stories, our concerns, our questions, and our struggles, and sharing how we worked through these issues, we model faith for our children.

## Connect Children and Teens to the Community

Meet teens' hunger for connection by encouraging their participation in the faith community. A sense of belonging is a very strong bond for children. They need the experience of being accepted, welcomed, and supported by the community. Youth need an experience of being able to trust others around them. Parents should encourage youth's participation in appropriate parish activities, including the parish youth ministry programs. Here young people can connect with their peers and create a positive peer group. Equally important, they can also connect with other caring, faith-filled adults. Surrounding our children with adults who practice their faith is especially important during their adolescence. In a sense it is creating a healthy "village" for our teens. This is an important experience of affiliation. Parents model this connection through their own involvement in the life of the faith community.

## Doing Faith

One of the most important characteristics of youth spirituality is their need to "do faith." Acting because of one's faith is a powerful experience. Participating in community religious practices like Sunday Mass, a public Stations of the Cross, a youth retreat, or a public teen pilgrimage are important opportunities to witness to one's faith. Perhaps the most powerful experience of doing faith is involvement in justice and service projects. Serving in soup kitchens, participating in a work camp, working in shelter programs or community emergency outreach centers, tutoring children, or visiting nursing homes have a very significant impact on teens' faith. This experience becomes even more powerful when teens and their parents share the experience together.

## Achieve Religious Literacy

In addition to the trusting and doing dimensions of faith, we also need to foster our youth's believing dimension. Children need to know the traditions, creed, teachings, and stories of the community. They need to know the story of Jesus and the Gospel message. They also need to know what it means to be a Catholic—or whatever their particular denomination. Young people need to know how to participate in the rituals and worship of the church. Of course, young people need to learn this in a way that is age appropriate, using sound methodology and creative approaches. Youth want to know, even when they are searching and challenging. The faith community needs to be a place where young people can bring their questions and search with others for answers that make sense, meet their needs, and provide meaning and purpose in their lives. We should encourage and support our children's participation in parish religious education programs, youth ministry, and sacramental preparation programs.

We need to remember, however, that education in one's faith is a lifelong process. We need to model, by our own willingness to continue learning about our faith, that there is always a deeper understanding of faith to be gained. In those Catholic dioceses where the sacrament of confirmation is celebrated during the middle or high school years, there is a temptation to consider confirmation as a sacrament of graduation. Parents sometimes portray an attitude that once their children are confirmed, they no longer have to participate in religious education because their understanding of faith is complete. Parents are often tempted to bargain with their children, trading off their further attendance at religious education programs for their participation in confirmation. Parish coordinators of religious education and youth ministry are challenged to develop programs that are interesting, relevant, and meaningful, even as we are challenged to encourage our children's ongoing involvement in parish programs.

> **We can greatly influence our teen's experience at Sunday Mass or worship by our level of participation. If we demonstrate an attitude that our attendance at Mass is solely from obligation, then our young people certainly cannot be blamed for not wanting to attend.**

## Prayer Experiences

Young people need to experience prayer as the outpouring of their relationship with a God who cares about them, loves them, and wants to communicate with them. There are two dimensions to prayer, remembering the first name and last name of faith. Youth need to pray in their own language, using their own music and symbols, and in their own space. Many teens say they experience

God most often in creation; e.g., at the ocean, in sunsets, or at the mountains, and in their rooms while listening to music. During the searching style of faith, young people might say, "Why do I have to go to church to pray, I can pray to God in my own room?" This reflects the first name of faith—they are establishing their own personal relationship with God. This dimension needs to be affirmed and supported. Teens really do have to develop their own understanding of God.

The last name of faith, though, is the communal or family name. Young people also belong to a faith community and share that community's understanding of God, their traditions, their rituals, and their ways of praying. Young people should be assisted in understanding and participating in the communal worship. We can greatly influence our teen's experience at Sunday Mass or worship by our level of participation. If we demonstrate an attitude that our attendance at Mass is solely from obligation, then our young people certainly cannot be blamed for not wanting to attend. If we are "Christmas and Easter" Christians, attending only on the important holy days, then should we expect anything more from our children? If we race to be the first out of the parking lot after church, how can our children think church is important?

Young people need both personal and communal experiences of prayer. They should be encouraged to pray on their own, in their words, using their music and symbols, and even writing their own prayers and spiritual poems. They should also be encouraged to participate with the faith community in worship experiences. This both/and approach to the personal and communal dimension, the first and last name of faith, fosters young people's relationship with God and deepens their faith.

So, when children say "Why do I have to go to church?" an appropriate response might be, "Because our family belongs to this church and we have a responsibility as members of the community to pray together with the other members of the church."

### Gathering Experiences
Young people have this hunger for connection; they want and need to belong. Even as they are struggling with their personal identity, they enter into relationships. They join clubs and teams, develop school spirit, follow local sports teams, and join community

organizations like Scouting, 4-H, volunteer fire departments, and the like. Young people want to be part of something bigger—and this is also true for their faith development. In fact, this desire or hunger to belong is especially important for their faith identity.

In a society that seems to give so many mixed messages about religion, young people find themselves struggling with belonging to a church, or acknowledging participating in church. Coming together with other young people who share the same faith—or at least a similar faith—is very important. These gathering experiences provide much needed support for children's growth in faith.

These gathering experiences begin with the local church youth ministry program. Young people need to gather with their peers right in their own church. They need opportunities to build community with their peers, to feel connected with other "faithing" youth, and to interact with caring, believing adults. We should advocate for local youth ministry programs if our church does not provide such opportunities.

However, gathering experiences move beyond the local church. Coming together with other young people at diocesan youth rallies, regional youth events, and national youth conferences give youth a sense of belonging to something bigger. In 2008, 223,000 Catholic young people traveled to Sydney, Australia, for World Youth Day with Pope Benedict XVI. This global gathering, started by Pope John Paul II, was held in the USA in 1993, in Denver, Colorado, and now occurs every two or three years, connecting young people with their peers from around the world. In our country, over 21,000 young people attended the biennial 2009 National Catholic Youth Conference in Kansas City. Truly, young people felt that they belonged to something bigger and something universal, and this experience of church continues to provide support and encouragement for those young people in attendance.

Gathering experiences are communal events, creating a sense of belonging to the family of faith, and fostering their "last name" of faith. However, these experiences also foster youth's personal journey of faith—their "first name" of faith. Gathering experiences provide youth with the opportunity to clarify and celebrate their personal faith, even as they experience belonging to something bigger than themselves.

*Scriptures of Their Own Lives*

Young people are searching for a personal understanding of God, their first name of faith, reflecting their hunger for the holy. As they do so, they must be able and encouraged to look for God's presence in their personal, lived experiences. Young people should be assisted in naming their experiences of a God who is active and present in their lives. God does not wait to be invited into the lives of young people. God takes the initiative and is present, but waits to be identified or named. Many young people need the language to help them understand and express their experiences of God.

Parents, and other caring, faith-filled adults, can assist young people in experiencing God's presence in their joys and sorrows, their hopes and dreams, and in their day to day life. Of course this requires that we have the language to name the presence of God in our own lives! We can ask our teenagers where they experience God, where they pray best, where they feel joy and sorrow, for God is present there. And we can share our experiences. The following are sample questions that parents can use with teenagers with regard to faith and religion.

- Where do you most experience the presence of God?
- Where do you pray best? When do you pray?
- What is the best part of belonging to our parish? What is the one thing you would change about our parish?
- On a scale of 1 to 10, how important is going to Mass on Sunday for you? What makes it a _____ (2, 5, 7, etc.)?
- Have you ever had an experience where your faith was really tested?
- Have you ever had an experience where your faith was really helpful to you?
- What most confuses you about faith and God?
- What church teaching most confuses you?
- How is your faith different now from when you were in grade school?
- What experiences, places, or persons have really fostered your growth in faith?

Parents can develop more questions as they speak with their teenagers about faith and religion. This faith sharing is an important task because young people will never understand the Hebrew-Christian Scriptures until they can read the Scriptures of their own lives. Therein, young people experience the God who is always active and present. And we should be open to having our own understanding of God challenged and perhaps deepened by our teenagers' experience of God. Young people often have very powerful experiences of God and they can enrich our faith, if there is a relationship that enables them to share these experiences with us.

### Power of Good Memories

As stated earlier, one of my favorite posters says, "There are only two things we can give our children that last: the first is roots and the second is wings." Many young people move through the searching style of faith, challenging the beliefs and practices of their parents and their church, and some even move away from regular participation and association with the institutional church. This is a time of "wings" for youth, a time for stretching and flying and experimenting—not only in terms of faith, but also in terms of finding themselves, deciding on their important values, entering into relationships, and making decisions about their future. And though all of these processes seem to take young people away from home, parents, and church, if we have provided an anchor, if we have provided "roots," then the flying is not nearly so frightening for our children, or for us.

These roots are established first in the family, in their relationship with us. Teens will remember the care, concern, and support they have experienced at home. They will remember the freedom to ask hard questions and to have different answers than their parents. They will remember how their questions and differing opinions were listened to respectfully, even as they heard their parents' beliefs and faith stories.

Roots are also teens' memories of caring, believing adult role models who expressed love and concern for them and their memory of a welcoming and supportive community of believers who invited them into their midst and encouraged their active participation. Roots are youth's memory of those times when they experienced God because others were visible signs of God's love for them.

The memories that young people have of belonging to a worshipping community, of putting their faith in action through service to others, of praying at home and with their church, of gathering with their peers in shared faith experiences—such memories are powerful. These memories will sustain young people as they deal with the sometimes harsh realities of life and as they struggle to develop their "last name of faith." These memories, these roots, give young people something to come back home to.

# Conclusion

An important caution to acknowledge is that implementing all of the suggestions and strategies described in the previous chapters does not guarantee a perfect relationship between parents and their teenagers. There will always be problems, tensions, and conflicts. We will make mistakes, and our children will make mistakes as well. We will get frustrated, even angry with our children. And they, in return, will be distant and withdrawn at times. But if we act out of love, if we clearly speak of the affection we feel for each member of our family, then we will survive the rough times. Skills will never substitute for a lack of love in our families, but good parenting skills will provide more avenues to express the love we feel for our children and teenagers.

We have to keep perspective, looking at our long term relationship with our children. We have to remember that someday we will be friends with our children. As our children grow older, more mature, and more independent, we need to affirm them for who they are now and for who they are becoming. Indeed, children and teenagers will be a blessing to us, and that will make all our efforts worthwhile.

# Appendix

## *10 Ways to Get Along with Parents*

*(As developed by Shannon McCarty, the author's daughter.)*

1.  Treat your parents as you want them to treat you. Even though it sounds pretty basic, if you want to be treated with respect and fairness, then we have to treat our parents the same way.

2.  Remember, parents are people too. That means they are human, they make mistakes, they loose their temper, they say things they do not necessarily mean. And they want to do their best, especially in raising their children.

3.  Handle the ordinary and the special will take care of itself. If we handle our normal curfews, chores, and school responsibilities, when something special comes up, we have a better chance to have the rules relaxed.

4.  It is okay to call time-out during family arguments. If you or your parents get really emotional during arguments—and that is when we say things we do not really mean—then agree to call time-out, and come back to the issue when everyone has cooled down.

5.  At least once a day, talk to your parents. Communication begins with a willingness to just talk. Parents get nervous when they feel out of touch with their children. So each day, just talk to them about things going on at school, or with your friends, or at your church group.

6.  Plan escape routes. Everyone gets into difficult situations; whether on a date, at a party, or just out with friends. So think about your options, in case something happens. Handling ourselves in difficult situations is a sign of maturity and responsibility.

7.  Agree on the basics. Talk with your parents about curfews, school expectations, household chores, driving with friends, and other issues, rather than relying on mind reading. Perhaps you can renegotiate the basics on your birthday, so as you get older, you gain more rights and responsibilities.

8.  Tell your parents that they are doing a good job. Parents get very little training on how to be good parents. It is more like trial and error. You will really surprise them by telling them they are doing okay.

9. Try to become friends with your parents. As strange as it sounds, when we get older we will be friends with our parents. So begin being friendly, talking with them, and sharing some time together.

10. Learn how to say "I am sorry." It is a sign of maturity to admit when we are wrong about something or at fault. Also, we have a better chance of convincing our parents when we are right.

# *Survey on Parent-Teen Relationships*

*This exercise should be completed by parents and their teenagers separately, then they can compare their responses. Circle your response.*

## For Teenagers

Yes  No  1.   Do your parents wait until you are through talking before having their say?

Yes  No  2.   Does your family do things as a group?

Yes  No  3.   Do your parents respect your opinions?

Yes  No  4.   Do your parents tend to lecture too much?

Yes  No  5.   Do you discuss your personal problems with either of your parents?

Yes  No  6.   Do your parents talk to you as if you were much younger than you are?

Yes  No  7.   Do your parents show interest in your activities?

Yes  No  8.   Do you and either parent discuss matters of sex?

Yes  No  9.   Do your parents trust you?

Yes  No  10.  Do you find it hard to say what you feel at home?

Yes  No  11.  Do your parents have confidence in your abilities?

Yes  No  12.  Do your parents consider your ideas before making decisions affecting you?

Yes  No  13.  Do your parents explain their reasons for the decisions they make regarding you?

Yes  No  14.  Do you and your parents try to see one another's side of things?

Yes  No  15.  Do you help your parents understand you by telling them how you think and feel?

***Bonus:***  In light of your answers to the questions above, rate your relationship with your parents.

_____ very good _____ good _____ fair _____ poor

***Bonus:***  Think of three constructive ideas on how to improve your relationship with your parents. Write them here.

## For Parents

Yes No 1.   Do your teenagers wait until you are through talking before having their say?

Yes No 2.   Does your family do things as a group?

Yes No 3.   Do your teenagers respect your opinions?

Yes No 4.   Do you tend to lecture your teenagers too much?

Yes No 5.   Do your teenagers discuss their personal problems with either parent?

Yes No 6.   Do you find yourself talking to your teenagers as if they were much younger than they really are?

Yes No 7.   Do your teenagers show much interest in your activities?

Yes No 8.   Do your teenagers discuss matters of sex with either parent?

Yes No 9.   Do you trust your teenagers?

Yes No 10.   Do your teenagers share how they feel at home?

Yes No 11.   Do you have confidence in your teenagers' abilities?

Yes No 12.   Do you consider your teenagers' ideas when making decisions affecting them?

Yes No 13.   Do you explain your reasons for decisions you make regarding them?

Yes No 14.   Do you and your teenagers try to see one another's side of things?

Yes No 15.   Do your teenagers help you understand them by telling you how they think and feel?

***Bonus:*** In light of your answers to the questions above, rate your relationship with your teenagers?

     \_\_\_\_\_ very good \_\_\_\_\_ good \_\_\_\_\_ fair \_\_\_\_\_ poor

***Bonus:*** Think of three constructive ideas on how to improve your relationship with your teenagers. Write them here.

# The ABCs of Showing Love

*(Adapted from Group Publishing, Inc. Used with permission.)*

*This exercise can be completed by both teenagers and parents and then the responses shared. When two parents are completing this exercise, they should do it separately before sharing their responses.*

## For Teenagers

*Below are many different ways of showing love to parents. Rate yourself on how often you show love in these ways. (O = often; S = sometimes; H = hardly ever; N = never).*

_____ I ask my parents how I can help.

_____ I give my parents flowers.

_____ I try to understand my parents' viewpoint.

_____ I thank my parents for their help.

_____ I talk to my parents about things that interest them.

_____ I do fun things with my parents.

_____ I listen to my parents.

_____ I tell my parents that I love them.

_____ I send notes or cards to my parents, on more than birthdays.

_____ I spend special time alone with Mom or Dad.

_____ I pray for my parents.

_____ I let my parents know they are special to me.

_____ I speak to my parents with respect.

_____ I tell my parents I appreciate them.

_____ I hug my Mom or Dad.

_____ I thank my parents for supporting our family.

_____ I forgive my parents when they make a mistake.

_____ I celebrate special times with my parents.

_____ I obey the rules my parents set.

_____ I spend time doing things with my parents because I want to.

# Scoring

*Now score yourself according to how many ways you checked O or S.*

14 to 20  Bravo! You really know how to let your parents know you care! Keep it up!

7 to 14  Good work! It sounds like you know how to show love to your parents. But you could stand to do it more often or in a greater variety of ways. Try three new ways this week.

0 to 6  Ouch! You need to work on showing love more. Pick out two new ways to show love each week for the next three weeks, and give them a try. Find ways that are comfortable for you, and meaningful to you and your parents.

## For Parents

*Below are many different ways of showing love to your teenagers. Rate yourself on how often you show love in these ways (O = often; S = sometimes; H = hardly ever; N = never).*

_____ I ask my teenagers how I can help them.

_____ I give my teenagers flowers.

_____ I try to understand my teenagers' viewpoint.

_____ I thank my teenagers for their help.

_____ I talk to my teenagers about things that interest them.

_____ I do fun things with my teenagers.

_____ I listen to my teenagers.

_____ I tell my teenagers that I love them.

_____ I send notes or cards to my teenagers, on more than birthdays.

_____ I spend special time alone with each of my teenagers.

_____ I pray for my teenagers.

_____ I let my teenagers know they are special to me.

_____ I tell my teenagers that I appreciate them.

_____ I hug my teenagers.

_____ I thank my teenagers for their contributions to our family.

_____ I forgive my teenagers when they make a mistake.

_____ I talk to my teenagers about the rules we set for them.

_____ I spend time doing things with my teenagers because I want to.

## Scoring

*Now score yourself according to how many ways you checked O or S.*

14 to 20  Bravo! You really know how to let your teenagers know you care. Keep it up!

7 to 13   Good work! It sounds like you know how to show love to your teenagers. But you could stand to do it more often or in a greater variety of ways. Try three ways this week.

0 to 6    Ouch! You need to work on showing love more. Pick out two new ways to show love each week for the next three weeks, and give them a try. Find ways that are comfortable for you, and meaningful to you and your teenagers.

# *Parent-Teen Conflict Resolution*

Conflict is a part of every close human relationship. When resolved respectfully, conflict is actually healthy because it promotes communication and yields solutions which work for everyone. Working at resolving conflict also communicates to your teenagers that you take them seriously and respect their feelings and opinions. Conflict involves two important dimensions: feelings and content or the issue causing the conflict. Successful resolution fosters a ventilating of the feelings and a discussion of the issue.

*The following suggestions will help you to "fight fair" as you work through conflict with your teenagers.*

## Rules for Fighting Fair

1. Realize that your teenagers are no longer children and therefore they are capable of reasoning in a more adult way. So, start by stating your belief that together you and your teen can resolve the problem.

2. Ask nonblaming questions to clarify the issue. An important step is spending time in naming or identifying the real issue.

3. Listen to your teen's point of view and realize that we all see things differently.

4. Share your feelings honestly about the issue, and encourage your teenagers to express their feelings, but watch for "fouls."

5. Stick to the issue. Do not dredge up past hurts or problems.

6. When you have been wrong, admit it. Ask for forgiveness.

7. Be willing to explore compromises. Avoid a win-lose resolution, which creates negative feelings and really does not create an effective resolution.

8. Do not give up until you have come to some resolution.

9. Set a time to discuss how the resolution is going and to see if it needs revisiting.

---

**Fouls Which Block the Process**

| Name Calling | Blaming | Physical Violence |
| Yelling | Threatening | Obscenities |
| Rolling Eyes | Insults | Using the "Silent Treatment" |

**Exercise 5**

# *Do Not Say . . . Do Say!*

*This exercise enables parents to identify sentences and statements which either hinder ("Do Not Say") or foster ("Do Say") effective relationships. Circle any you have used in conversation with your teenagers. After you are finished, ask your teenager(s) to star those they have heard. Compare your lists and share your reactions.*

## Do Not Say . . .

- "As long as you are under my roof . . ."
- "Your room is such a mess. How can you live like that?"
- "Haven't you finished your homework yet?"
- "Who was that on the phone?"
- "Go ask your father (mother)."
- "You are the oldest and should be more responsible."
- "Money does not grow on trees."
- "Good things do not come easy."
- "When I was your age . . ."
- "You are old enough to know better."
- "That is what you get for waiting until the last moment."
- "Because I said so."
- "I do not need a reason."
- "I love you, but . . ."
- "What is wrong with teenagers today?"

## Do Say . . .

- "Because we are a family . . ."
- "I love you."
- "You are doing a good job of growing up."
- "I believe in you."
- "That sounds like a difficult decision that you have to make."
- "I really like your friends."
- "I like the way you handled . . ."
- "You do a good job of budgeting your time."
- "You are really helpful around the house."
- "You make good decisions."
- "You look very nice today."
- "I appreciate your going to church with us. I know it is not easy at times."
- "Thank you."
- "I am proud of you."
- "I do not understand . . ., can you help me?"

**Exercise 6**

# *Youth-Parent Questionnaires*

*(from "Helping Youth Decide" by the National Association of State Boards of Education, 1986. Arlington, Virginia. Used with permission.)*

*Parents and teenagers should fill out their respective questionnaires separately and then share their responses.*

## Youth Questionnaire

1.  I spend about _____ hours a week talking with my (mother) (father).

2.  When something is bothering me, my (mother) (father) usually: (check the one that comes closest)

    a.  assumes my problems cannot be all that serious.

    b.  figures it out before I say anything.

    c.  is willing to take the time to listen.

    d.  goes overboard and lectures me. I know (she) (he) means well but it never helps.

3.  When I ask for permission to do something, my (mother) (father):

    a.  usually says "yes" because (she)(he) trusts me.

    b.  usually says "yes," but I wonder if (she) (he) is even listening.

    c.  questions me and sometimes really invades my privacy.

    d.  usually says "no" because (she)(he) does not trust me.

    e.  other _____

    _____

    _____

4.  My best friends are: (list names) _____

    _____

    _____

5.   My most frustrating experience of the past few weeks was:_____

_____

_____

_____

_____

6.   My most frustrating experience with my (mother) (father) in the past few weeks was: _____

_____

_____

_____

_____

7.   One of the things about me that makes my (mother) (father) feel proud is: _____

_____

_____

_____

_____

8.   One of the things that bothers my (mother) (father) about me is:

_____

_____

_____

_____

9.  The biggest decision I have ever made on my own is: _____

    _____

    _____

    _____

    _____

10. A mutually agreeable decision that my (mother) (father) and I
    have made together within the last month is: _____

    _____

    _____

    _____

    _____

## Parent Questionnaire

1. Right now, I spend _____hours a week talking with my (son) (daughter).

2. When something is bothering (him) (her) I usually: (check the one that comes the closest)

   a. assume that the problem cannot be all that serious.

   b. am sensitive to the fact that there is a problem—and I am often right about that.

   c. take the time to listen.

   d. become deeply involved—giving freely of my experience and advice.

3. When my (son) (daughter) asks for permission to do something, I: (check the one that comes closest)

   a. usually say "yes" because I trust (him)(her).

   b. usually say "yes" because (he)(she) is going to do it anyway.

   c. want more information and may want to check things out for myself.

   d. usually say "no" because (he)(she) has such a poor track record.

   e. other: _____

4. My (son's) (daughter's) best friends are: (list names) _____

   _____

   _____

   _____

   _____

5. (His) (Her) most frustrating experience in the past few weeks was: _____

   _____

   _____

   _____

   _____

6. The most frustrating experience (he) (she) had with me in the past few weeks was:_____

_____

_____

_____

_____

7. One thing about my (son) (daughter) that I am proud of is:

_____

_____

_____

_____

8. One thing that bothers me about (him) (her) is: _____

_____

_____

_____

_____

9. The biggest decision my (son) (daughter) has ever made on (his) (her) own is: _____

_____

_____

_____

_____

10. A mutually agreeable decision my (son) (daughter) and I have made together within the last month is: _____

_____

_____

_____

_____

# *I Think We Would Get Along Better If...*

*(Based on* "What the Kids Say . . ." *by Audrey Taylor*. Vision & Challenge, Vol. 2, No. 1, Fall 1994, *pp. 23-30. Copyright © Center for Ministry Development, 1994. All rights reserved. Used with permission.)*

*After completing the appropriate reflection sheet, parents and teenagers compare their responses.*

## Teenager Letter

Dear Parent,

As your teenager, I think we would get along better if you would: (circle your top seven pieces of advice)

1. Admit it when you are wrong.

2. Spend some time with me one-on-one.

3. Listen to me. Really listen to me. Do not lecture me.

4. Do not compare me to my brothers and sisters.

5. Do not say, "When I was your age . . ."

6. Trust me more. And do not always give me the third degree when I want to go somewhere with my friends.

7. Appreciate me more. Say "thank you" more often instead of taking me for granted.

8. Stop bugging me about grades and studying.

9. Allow me my privacy. Do not listen in on my phone conversations, check my mail . . ..

10. Laugh more.

11. Stop complaining about my music.

12. Compliment me more. Give me some praise once in a while.

13. Do not compare me to other teenagers.

14. Tell me about sex and how to handle it.

15. Stay home more often.

16. Pray more . . . for me and with me.

17. Watch TV less.

18. Spend less time on work and more time on the family.

## Parent Letter

Dear Teenager,

As your parent, I think we would get along better if you would: (circle your top seven pieces of advice)

1. Admit it when you are wrong.
2. Stay home more often.
3. Listen to me. Really listen to me. Do not turn me off.
4. Care more about your brothers and sisters. Fight less.
5. Do not say, "You just do not understand me."
6. Be worthy of my trust. Do not lie to me.
7. Appreciate me more. Say "thank you" more often instead of just taking me for granted.
8. Put more effort into your grades and studying.
9. Do not overdo your privacy. Come out of your room and share with the family once in a while.
10. Laugh more.
11. Turn down the volume on your music.
12. Compliment me more. Give me some praise once in a while.
13. Do not compare me to other parents.
14. Ask me more about sex and how to handle it.
15. Stay home more often.
16. Pray more . . . for me and with me.
17. Watch TV less.
18. Clean up your room.

**Exercise 8**

# *Trustworthiness*

*(Adapted from GROUP Publishing. Used with permission.)*

*Parents and teenagers should complete their respective exercises and then compare responses and scores.*

## For Teenagers

How trustworthy are you? Circle the appropriate number for each of the following areas. Then add the numbers and read the scoring table to see what your score means.

1. How often do you come home by curfew?

| Always | | Sometimes | | Never |
|--------|---|-----------|---|-------|
| 5 | 4 | 3 | 2 | 1 |

2. How often do you do all your chores on time?

| Always | | Sometimes | | Never |
|--------|---|-----------|---|-------|
| 5 | 4 | 3 | 2 | 1 |

3. How often do you do all the homework you are supposed to?

| Always | | Sometimes | | Never |
|--------|---|-----------|---|-------|
| 5 | 4 | 3 | 2 | 1 |

4. How often do you let parents know your plans?

| Always | | Sometimes | | Never |
|--------|---|-----------|---|-------|
| 5 | 4 | 3 | 2 | 1 |

5. How often are you careful as a driver (or as a passenger with other teen drivers)?

| Always | | Sometimes | | Never |
|--------|---|-----------|---|-------|
| 5 | 4 | 3 | 2 | 1 |

6. How often do you tell the full truth to your parents?

| Always | | Sometimes | | Never |
|--------|---|-----------|---|-------|
| 5 | 4 | 3 | 2 | 1 |

Total Points: _____

---

**Scoring**

| | |
|---|---|
| 25-30 | Congratulations! You deserve to be trusted. |
| 16-24 | You know how to be trustworthy—keep up the good work. |
| 11-15 | You have got some work to do. Try to be more consistent in your responsibilities. |
| 6-10 | Do you wonder why your parents do not trust you? Start being more responsible and give them a reason to trust you. |

## For Parents

*How is the level of trust and communication in your relationship with your teenager? Circle the appropriate number for each of the following areas. Then add the numbers and read the scoring table to see what the score means.*

1. How often do you reward your teen's responsibility by extending curfew or other freedoms?

   Always     Sometimes     Never
     5      4       3        2      1

2. How often do you respect your teen's privacy? (Their rooms, letters, diaries, phone calls)

   Always     Sometimes     Never
     5      4       3        2      1

3. How often do you show interest in your teen's school and other activities?

   Always     Sometimes     Never
     5      4       3        2      1

4. Do you know your teen's friends and their leisure time plans?

   Always     Sometimes     Never
     5      4       3        2      1

5. With clear expectations, how often do you allow your teen to borrow the car (or drive the car with you along)?

   Always     Sometimes     Never
     5      4       3        2      1

6. How often do you share your real feelings with your teen (Have you ever said "I am sorry" or "I am wrong")?

   Always     Sometimes     Never
     5      4       3        2      1

Total points: _____

---

### Scoring

| | |
|---|---|
| 25-30 | Congratulations! You are working hard at your relationship! |
| 16-24 | You are on the way, keep up the good work. |
| 11-15 | It would be good to work on communication in your family. |
| 6-10 | Communication and trust are a real issue in your family. |

# *Dinner Table Discussion*

*The following questions can be used as conversation starters. Parents should not take on the "authority" or "expert" role or dominate the conversation. These questions are stated in a general way: referring to "teenagers" and "their parents," rather than "you" and "in our family." Keeping the discussion general makes it less threatening and less personal and may initially foster a better discussion. Once the family is comfortable discussing various issues, the questions can be focused on their family, their teenagers, and their parents. Parents and teenagers are encouraged to create their own questions. Perhaps the family could designate one night each week as "Bring a Question Night" or "Hot Topic Night."*

1.  What are the three key issues, concerns, or problems facing teenagers today? What creates stress for teenagers? What are the issues for adults? What creates stress for parents today?

2.  What are the biggest sources of conflict at home for teenagers or with their parents?

3.  What one thing could parents do to get along better with their teenagers? What one thing could teenagers do to get along better with their parents?

4.  What do teenagers need from their parents today, in order to face all the pressures of growing up?

5.  What causes all the pressure for teenagers to drink alcohol today? Was there the same pressure when the parents were teenagers? What do some teenagers do to avoid the drinking, while still attending parties where drinking occurs?

6.  What is causing teenagers to engage in drug use today? What are the most popular drugs used in our neighborhood? How extensive is drug use in the schools? What was drug use like when the parents were teenagers? How can a teenager say "no" to drugs, without looking "weird?"

7.  Where do teenagers get most of their information about sex? What message does the media (TV shows, movies, advertisements) give about sexual relationships? Is there pressure today for teenagers to have sex? Where did parents get their information about sex when they were teenagers? Do teenagers today ever have "the talk" with their parents anymore?

8.  What qualities do teenagers look for in a relationship? What kind of person do they want to date? What is the "ideal date"? What was the "ideal date" when parents were teenagers?

9.  Is peer pressure as strong as the media says it is? What gives peer pressure such power to control behavior? How do teenagers handle peer pressure? What was peer pressure like when the parents were teens? What behavior(s) does/did peer pressure encourage?

10. How many teenagers go to church or are involved in church activities? What do teenagers like about their church? What do teenagers not like about their church? What changes would churches have to make in order to attract teenagers? When parents were teenagers did they go to church?

11. How would teenagers describe God? Where do teenagers pray best? When do teenagers most experience God's presence? What do teenagers think about Jesus? When parents were teenagers, how did they describe God? When did they pray? When do they pray now? How important is faith today?

12. What do teenagers like most about their school? Like least about their school? Who are the best teachers and what makes them the best? What are the favorite subjects? Worst subjects? What are the best extracurricular activities, organizations, and clubs?

13. What do teenagers think the world will be like in 5 years? 10 years? 25 years? What do teenagers most look forward to? Least look forward to? What is the best thing about becoming an adult? What is the worst thing about becoming an adult? When parents were teenagers, what did they think the future would be like?

14. Local current events: What do you think of the level of _____ (violence, poverty, homelessness, drug abuse, environmental pollution, etc.) in our country (city, community, neighborhood)? What seem to be the causes? What should our government do? What should the common citizens do? What were the issues when parents were teenagers?

15. International current events: What do you make of the situation in _____. What do you think is the issue? What should our government do? What were the international issues when parents were teenagers?

Exercise 10

# *Making Good Decisions: The DECIDE Approach*

*Decision making is one of the most critical skills for young people to develop. Described here is a step by step process for responsible decision making which can be applied to situations confronting our teenagers.*

**D**   **Define** the issue, question, or problem. Gather the facts about the situation and clearly name the decision to be made.

**E**   **Explore** the options and alternatives. Look at the various choices that will solve the problem.

**C**   **Consider** the consequences of each alternative. Consider the pros and cons, the advantages and disadvantages of each of the alternatives.

**I**   **Inquire** about other's opinions. Ask parents or other significant adults for their advice. Consider your personal values and morals, your faith stance, your church's teachings, and society's understanding of acceptable behavior.

**D**   **Decide** on the best course of action. Having considered all the facts, alternatives, consequences, and others' input, make the decision.

**E**   **Evaluate** your decision after having acted on it. Evaluate the consequences and make any necessary changes and modifications.

---

**Two Important Concepts for Decision Making**

- **Responsible decision making** refers to making decisions only after carefully considering the possible alternatives and consequences.
- **Accountability** refers to accepting the responsibility for the consequences of one's decisions. This includes the praise and congratulations when good decisions are made, as well as the results of poor decisions.